HMSO ✓
.48

HOME OFFICE
ANIMALS (SCIENTIFIC PROCEDURES) ACT 1986

Code of Practice

FOR THE HOUSING AND CARE OF ANIMALS IN DESIGNATED BREEDING AND SUPPLYING ESTABLISHMENTS

Presented pursuant to Act Eliz. II 1986 C.14 Section 21
(Animals (Scientific Procedures) Act 1986)

Ordered by the House of Commons to be printed
24 January 1995

London: HMSO

£8.95 net

Contents

	Paragraph	Page
PART 1		
1. INTRODUCTION		1
INSPECTORS	1.3	1
ANIMALS PROCEDURES COMMITTEE	1.4	1
CODES OF PRACTICE	1.5	1
THIS CODE OF PRACTICE	1.7	2
APPLICATION OF CODE OF PRACTICE	1.11	3
2. HOUSING AND ENVIRONMENT		4
INTRODUCTION		4
THE ANIMAL HOUSE	2.12	5
SECURITY	2.14	6
ANIMAL ROOMS	2.15	6
TREATMENT ROOMS	2.25	7
SERVICE AND SUPPORT FACILITIES	2.28	7
FACILITIES FOR STAFF	2.33	7
STAFFING	2.35	8
TRAINING	2.36	8
THE NAMED VETERINARY SURGEON	2.39	8
THE ENVIRONMENT	2.40	9
TEMPERATURE	2.41	9
RELATIVE HUMIDITY	2.46	10
VENTILATION	2.47	10
LIGHTING	2.51	10
NOISE	2.52	10
EMERGENCY ALARM AND STANDBY SYSTEMS	2.54	11
3. ANIMAL CARE AND HEALTH		12
INTRODUCTION		12
RESPONSIBILITY FOR ANIMALS	3.4	12
SOURCES OF ANIMALS	3.5	12
RECEPTION	3.8	13
DESPATCH	3.10	13

	Paragraph	Page
TRANSPORT	3.11	13
ACCLIMATISATION AND QUARANTINE	3.18	14
CARE OF ANIMALS		14
ANIMAL ACCOMMODATION	3.19	1
BEDDING AND NESTING MATERIAL	3.28	15
FOOD	3.29	16
WATER	3.32	16
ENVIRONMENTAL ENRICHMENT	3.34	16
HANDLING	3.38	17
CLEANING	3.39	17
ANIMAL HEALTH		17
BREEDING RECORDS	3.44	18

PART 2

INDIVIDUAL SPECIES REQUIREMENTS

4. MICE, RATS,. HAMSTERS

INTRODUCTION	4.1	19
THE ENVIRONMENT	4.2	20
ANIMAL CARE AND HEALTH	4.8	21

5. RABBITS

INTRODUCTION	5.1	25
THE ENVIRONMENT	5.2	25
ANIMAL CARE AND HEALTH	5.7	26

6. GUINEA PIGS

INTRODUCTION	6.1	28
THE ENVIRONMENT	6.2	28
ANIMAL CARE AND HEALTH	6.7	29

7. DOGS

INTRODUCTION	7.1	31
THE ENVIRONMENT	7.2	31
ANIMAL CARE AND HEALTH	7.7	32

8. CATS

| INTRODUCTION | 8.1 | 35 |

	Paragraph	Page
THE ENVIRONMENT	8.1	35
ANIMAL CARE AND HEALTH	8.7	36

9. NON HUMAN PRIMATES

INTRODUCTION	9.1	38
ACQUISITION OF ANIMALS	9.2	38
RECEIPT AND DESPATCH OF ANIMALS	9.3	39
ANIMAL IDENTIFICATION	9.5	40
ANIMAL HEALTH	9.6	40
BREEDING PROGRAMMES	9.7	41
INDIVIDUAL SPECIES REQUIREMENTS	9.9	42
– NEW WORLD MONKEYS (*Platyrrhini*)	9.9	42
– MARMOSETS (*Callithrix*)	9.10	42
– TAMARINS (*Saguinus*)	9.22	45
– OWL MONKEY (*Aotus*)	9.24	45
– SQUIRREL MONKEYS (*Saimiri*)	9.27	46
– OLD WORLD MONKEYS (*Cercopithecidae*)	9.30	46

10. QUAIL

INTRODUCTION	10.1	50
THE ENVIRONMENT	10.2	50
ANIMAL CARE AND HEALTH	10.6	51

11. BIBLIOGRAPHY | | 53 |

CODE OF PRACTICE FOR THE HOUSING AND CARE OF ANIMALS IN DESIGNATED BREEDING AND SUPPLYING ESTABLISHMENTS
(issued under Section 21)

Part 1

1 INTRODUCTION

1.1. The Animals (Scientific Procedures) Act 1986 regulates "any experimental or other scientific procedure applied to an animal which may have the effect of causing that animal pain, suffering, distress or lasting harm".

1.2. The Act came into effect on January 1987, and during the period until 1st January 1990 its provisions were progressively brought into force. Section 7 of the Act, which pertains to Breeding and Supplying Establishments was brought into force on 1st January 1990.

Inspectors

1.3. Section 18 of the Act empowers the Home Secretary to appoint Inspectors; sets out their duties to visit establishments and advise and report to the Secretary of State; and empowers Inspectors to order the killing of an animal if it is considered to be undergoing excessive suffering.

Animals Procedures Committee

1.4. Section 19 of the Act establishes the Animal Procedures Committee and sets out its constitution. Section 20 of the Act lays down that it is the duty of the Committee to advise the Home Secretary, having "regard both to the legitimate requirements of science and industry and to the protection of animals against avoidable suffering and unnecessary use in scientific procedures".

Codes of Practice

1.5. Under Section 21 of the Act, the Home Secretary is required to "issue codes of practice as to the care of protected animals and their use for regulated procedures and may approve such codes issued by other persons" and to consult the Animal Procedures Committee before publishing such a Code.

1.6. This Code of Practice is issued under Section 21. Section 21 (4) says that a "failure on the part of any person to comply with any provision of a code ... shall not of itself render that person liable to criminal or civil proceedings but ... any such code shall be admissible in evidence in any such proceedings ... and if any of its provisions appears to the court ... to be relevant ... it shall be taken into account" in determining the outcome of the case.

This Code of Practice

1.7. In 1989 Parliament endorsed the Code of Practice for the housing and care of animals used in scientific procedures (1), which was closely based on the Royal Society and the Universities Federation for Animal Welfare (RS/UFAW) Guidelines (2). This Code applies to designated scientific procedure establishments but **not** to places designated solely as breeding or supplying establishments.

1.8. The present Code applies to all species of animals listed in Schedule 2 to the Act maintained in designated breeding and/or supplying establishments.

1.9. It is issued following extensive consultations within the scientific community, with laboratory animal breeding organisations and with organisations concerned with the welfare of animals.

The Laboratory Animals Breeders Association (LABA) Guidelines (3) on the care and housing of animals bred for scientific purposes, which were prepared in consultation with the Association of the British Pharmaceutical Industry (ABPI), British Laboratory Animal Veterinary Association (BLAVA), Institute of Animal Technology (IAT), and the Laboratory Animal Science Association (LASA), have been used in breeding establishments for a number of years. As these standards have been found to be acceptable in terms of animal behaviour, welfare and productivity these have been used as the basis for the standards in this Code of Practice.

The recommendations on housing and care of laboratory animals detailed in Annex II of European Directive 86/609 EEC (4) and in Appendix A of the European Convention for the Protection of Vertebrate Animals used for Experimental and other Scientific Purposes (5) have been given due consideration.

Representatives of ABPI, BLAVA, IAT, LABA, LASA, Royal Society for the Prevention of Cruelty to Animals (RSPCA) and UFAW, and a number of invited experts were invited to consider suitable standards of housing and care for breeding animals. The recommendations of this group were based on an agreed consensus of present knowledge and practices and following due consideration of existing guidelines. Differences from the requirements of the Code of Practice for animals used in scientific procedures reflect the special needs of breeding animals. This Code is very closely based on these recommendations, and has the support of those who participated in its formulation.

This Code has been endorsed by the Animal Procedures Committee.

1.10. Although some flexibility in interpretation of the recommendations may be permitted following consultation and with the agreement of the Inspector, for example to permit the introduction of innovative enriched housing systems, the quantitative standards which are included for cage dimensions or space allowances are set at the minimum acceptable level. Where facilities are not satisfactory a realistic (but not too extended) timetable for improvements will be set.

Application of the Code of Practice

1.11. This Code applies throughout the United Kingdom. In Great Britain it is administered by the Home Office. In Northern Ireland, it is administered by the Department of Health and Social Services. Where the Code speaks of the "Secretary of State" or "the Home Office" it means, in Northern Ireland, the Department of Health and Social Services.

1.12. As understanding of how best to care for animals evolves, the recommendations contained in this Code of Practice may need to be updated. The Secretary of State will keep this Code of Practice under review and will issue amendments as necessary.

2 HOUSING AND ENVIRONMENT

Introduction

2.1. The purpose of this Code of Practice is to establish minimum standards for the breeding, care and housing of laboratory animals in Designated Breeding and Supplying Establishments.

2.2. As breeding animals typically are maintained for longer periods than animals used on scientific procedures, particular attention is required to ensure that the environment provides for the animals' behavioural as well as physiological needs.

2.3. In breeding and supplying establishments, stock animals should be maintained, as far as is possible, in conditions suited to their subsequent scientific use. This minimises the introduction of avoidable variables, limits the need for lengthy acclimatisation periods, and maintains as far as is possible uniformity in the animals supplied.

2.4. In scientific work involving living animals, the most reliable results are likely to be obtained by using healthy animals that are well adapted to and not unduly stressed by their housing conditions. In quantitative assays or comparisons, precision is increased by any factors favouring increased uniformity in the animals to be used.

2.5. Article 5 in Directive 86/609 of the Council of the European Communities (4) requires Member States to ensure, as far as the general care and accommodation of animals is concerned:

> *"a. all experimental animals shall be provided with housing, an environment, at least some freedom of movement, food, water and care which are appropriate to their health and well being;*
>
> *b. any restriction on the extent to which an experimental animal can satisfy its physiological and ethological needs shall be limited to the absolute minimum;*
>
> *c. the environmental conditions in which experimental animals are bred, kept or used must be checked daily.*
>
> *d. the well-being and state of health of experimental animals shall be observed by a competent person to prevent pain or avoidable suffering, distress or lasting harm;*
>
> *e. arrangements are made to ensure that any defect or suffering discovered is eliminated as quickly as possible.*
>
> *For the implementation of the provisions of paragraphs a. and b. Member States shall pay regard to the guidelines (for accommodation and care) set out in Annex II".*

The relevant 1986 European Convention (5) details similar provisions of an advisory nature.

2.6. These principles have been borne in mind throughout the preparation of this Code.

2.7. In addition to the standards of care and husbandry set out in this Code of Practice, protected animals are subject to other controls. For example, the Protection of Animals Act 1911 (1912 Scotland); in Northern Ireland, the Welfare of Animals Act (NI) 1972 prohibits causing or permitting any unnecessary suffering. The Animal Health Act 1981 and Diseases of Animals (NI) Order 1981 apply in respect of notifiable diseases.

The Welfare of Animals during Transport Order 1992 provides standards for care of animals during transport.

2.8. Where animal facilities do not conform to the standards of this Code, a programme and timetable for upgrading will be agreed with the Home Office Inspector. Modifications necessary for the welfare of the animals will be made without delay. The requirements for accommodation and care in this Code are intended to set the minimum quantitative acceptable standards. New facilities must meet the standards, but except for cage sizes and space allowances which set minimum requirements, the standards are not intended to imply that absolute uniformity is in itself desirable. Any proposal to provide alternative standards must be justified. The use of higher standards is encouraged as is the introduction of novel environments and methods for improving the utilisation of available space to provide improved behavioural well-being.

Inspectors will consider as part of their enquiries, whether the facilities, or any proposed changes, are acceptable before making a recommendation to the Secretary of State on applications for certificates of designation or their amendment.

2.9. Only competent staff may be given unsupervised responsibility for the care and husbandry of animals. Those responsible for laboratory animals must be trained in their care and be familiar with the basic welfare requirements of their animals. They need to be aware of their legal and welfare responsibilities. They must appreciate also the importance of, and be competent in, correct animal handling, husbandry and restraint. They must be able to recognise signs of pain, distress and disease in animals in their care.

2.10. Appropriate training is essential to ensure that knowledge, skills and attitudes are instilled to provide for both the physiological and behavioural requirements of the animals (6).

2.11. Under the Health and Safety at Work etc. Act 1974, the person in charge of a unit is required to ensure that it is a safe place in which to work. Staff should be aware of the action to be taken in case of accident, fire or other emergencies, and of the potential existence of zoonotic organisms. Occupational asthma caused by exposure to laboratory animals is a proscribed disease. For further information, see Bibliography (7, 8, 9, 10).

THE ANIMAL HOUSE

2.12. An animal house shall provide a suitable environment, including any special requirements for exercise and social contact for the species to be housed, and should incorporate facilities sufficient for the activities carried out within it. When substantial alterations to the premises are proposed, the Inspector should be consulted at an early stage.

2.13. When siting an animal house, consideration should be given to the activities in the adjacent buildings and any effect these may have on the welfare of the animals. An animal facility forming part of a larger complex should be designed to be self-contained. Wild, stray or pet animals should not be able to gain entry to any part of the animal house, including stores and personnel areas. Special care is needed where drains and other services pierce the walls or floors to ensure that they have been adequately proofed against vermin (11).

Security

2.14. The animal house and its facilities should be designed to prevent animals escaping. It is also proving necessary to protect animal facilities against illegal entry by unauthorised persons. Advice should be sought and taken about security from Crime Prevention Officers from the local police or other experts during the design of new facilities or modifications of existing premises.

Animal Rooms

2.15. For the purpose of this Code, an animal room means the room normally used to house stock or breeding animals and animal treatment areas. Outside exercise areas will by definition not be subject to controls over ventilation, temperature and relative humidity. Likewise, environmental control in rooms providing permanent access to outside areas will necessarily be less precise than in rooms with only internal communications.

2.16. Animal rooms should be constructed of durable impervious materials, with easily cleanable surfaces which are resistant to attack from the chemicals used to clean or fumigate the rooms. Consideration should be given to the use of materials which are least likely to crack and craze. Floor finishes should be non-slip whether wet or dry. All joints between door frames and walls should be sealed.

2.17. Services should be installed in such a way that they are either buried within the fabric of the building, boxed in or clear of the wall surface for easy cleaning. When the fabric of the building is penetrated, the holes created should be sealed.

2.18. Design should take into account the fact that building maintenance may disturb animals. Whenever possible, services should be installed to be accessible from outside and with fittings that can be removed by the staff for maintenance or repair elsewhere. If possible, provision should be made for the addition of new services during the lifespan of the building, for instance by the insertion of spare ducting in the walls.

2.19. Animal rooms must be adequately ventilated. The stocking density for each room for each species likely to be housed should be calculated, and adjusted to match the performance of the ventilation system. Any smell of ammonia suggests overstocking, too little ventilation, inadequate cleaning, or a combination of these factors; the causes should be investigated and rectified.

2.20. Species that are incompatible, for example predator and prey, or animals requiring different environmental conditions or of different health status, should not be housed in the same room nor, in the case of predator and prey, within smell or sound.

2.21. Precautions should be taken in animal rooms to minimise the exposure of personnel to hazards which may arise from the incorrect handling of animals, for example bites and scratches, allergens and infections (8, 9).

2.22. There should be special provision to house animals that are ill or injured including, if necessary, facilities for isolation.

2.23. In institutions which are designated both as breeding and as scientific procedure establishments, breeding animals should normally be held separately from animals on procedures. Where breeding forms part of a regulated procedure authorised by a Project Licence, for example in the case of transgenic or harmful mutants, the standards set out in the Code of Practice for the Housing and Care of Animals used in Scientific Procedures (1) will generally apply.

According to the microbiological and genetic quality of animal desired, different levels of separation and physical barriers will be required between breeding and other areas.

2.24. Adequate arrangements should be provided for the receipt of incoming animals. Animals brought into an animal house should not put at risk animals which are already there. Space should be provided for acclimatisation and quarantine, where appropriate.

Treatment rooms

2.25. General and specialist veterinary treatment rooms should be provided as appropriate. Major surgery and euthanasia must not be performed in rooms where animals are normally housed.

2.26. Where surgery is to be performed, suitable operating facilities must be provided, including separate preparation areas for the animals, equipment and staff. Surgery will be carried out under appropriate clean or aseptic conditions in a designated operating room. There should be a post-operative recovery area.

2.27. All establishments should have access to facilities for diagnostic investigation, post-mortem examinations and the collection of samples for examination elsewhere.

Service areas and support facilities

2.28. The design and construction of service and circulation areas should normally be of the same standard as the animal rooms. The building should be planned to prevent cross-contamination between clean and dirty equipment. Corridors should be wide enough for easy movement of personnel and equipment, and should not be used for storage.

2.29. Service areas are subject to rough treatment and wall surfaces should be resistant to impact damage, with guard rails to protect walls and corners. Surfaces and corners should be easy to clean. Adequate floor drainage should be provided in wash areas, with sufficient ventilation to remove excess heat and humidity.

2.30. Stores must be separate from animal rooms. Adequate storage space should be provided for food, bedding, cages, cleaning materials and other items. Special facilities may be required for handling and storing chemicals.

2.31. Food and bedding stores should be clean, dry and vermin proof. In addition, food stores should be cool and sunless and well ventilated. Perishable foods should be stored in cold rooms, refrigerators or freezers.

2.32. A separate collection area should be provided for waste, prior to its disposal. Special arrangements should be made for handling carcasses (12).

Facilities for staff

2.33. Personnel facilities should include staff and record rooms, sufficient changing rooms, decontamination areas, first aid and toilet facilities and space for storing protective and outdoor clothing.

2.34. Animal care personnel may be present at times when normal catering facilities may not be available; special arrangements or facilities for meals may therefore be needed. Smoking, eating and drinking should be prohibited in all areas other than those staff areas specifically reserved for such activities.

Staffing

2.35. Sufficient staff must be available at all times to care for the animals, including during weekends, holiday periods and when the normal staff are absent e.g. due to sickness.

Training

2.36. Appropriate training of staff is essential to ensure that high standards of husbandry and care are provided (13).

The holder of the Certificate of Designation is responsible for ensuring that adequate training is provided for all animal care staff. This responsibility is commonly delegated to the named person in day-to-day care. The form and content of training will depend on the activities being carried out, although attendance at formal training courses is strongly recommended.

Training should include an introduction to the natural history and behaviour of the species which will illustrate their needs in a captive breeding system. Animal care staff should be trained to recognise normal behaviour, in order that any abnormalities can be identified at an early stage.

It is recommended that written husbandry, care and safety instructions be provided which may include reference to other relevant legislation, for example the Health and Safety at Work Act. Details of routine husbandry, breeding programmes, disposal of waste and carcasses, disease surveillance and control programmes should be maintained.

2.37. The Register of Animal Technicians maintained by the Institute of Animal Technology may be helpful in identifying individuals of suitable quality and status to fill posts of responsibility within the animal facility. Information on training and courses in laboratory animal science and technology are available from the Business and Technician Education Council, the Institute of Animal Technology, the Institute of Biology, and the Royal College of Veterinary Surgeons.

2.38. Animal care staff are expected, at all times, to have a caring and respectful attitude towards animals in their care, and must be trained to become proficient in their handling, restraint and husbandry.

The named veterinary surgeon

2.39. Under section 6(5)(b) of the 1986 Act, it is a requirement for certification as a designated establishment that there is a named veterinary surgeon to provide advice on the health and welfare of the animals. It is important that named veterinary surgeons have detailed knowledge of the needs of the species of laboratory animals on which they will provide advice. The Royal College of Veterinary Surgeons (RCVS) has published a Code of Practice for Named Veterinary Surgeons (NVS) (14). The RCVS expects veterinary surgeons accepting appointments as NVS to undertake specific training in order to extend their knowledge and thus meet their statutory role under the Animals (Scientific Procedures) Act 1986. The RCVS recommends that such veterinary surgeons should give serious consideration to attending courses specifically aimed at Named Veterinary

Surgeons and follow a line of post-graduate training leading to a higher qualification.

THE ENVIRONMENT

2.40. Housing restricts an animal's ability to exercise choice and, therefore, has to provide for as many of the animals' needs as can reasonably be met. The environmental needs of breeding animals are likely to differ from those of stock and experimental animals for four reasons:

1. Breeding animals typically have longer lives than those used in experiments and the female is exposed to the stresses of reproduction. Hence, particular attention needs to be given to designing an environment that takes account of the animal's behavioural as well as physical needs.

2. Animals give birth during the time of day when they are usually quiescent and will often seek or create a secure place for parturition and the raising of offspring; typically a nest or den in the case of rodents, cats, dogs and birds. Such behaviour is strongly motivated. The breeder should ensure that the animal's need for privacy is considered. This can be achieved by the provision of nesting material, nestboxes or a secluded and sheltered area within the pen or cage. Nesting material also allows the animal to partially control its own environment (e.g. noise, temperature and humidity). Given the means for controlling its own microenvironment, the permissible range of room temperatures may be wider than would otherwise be the case.

3. In some species when breeding stock are housed in social groups, subordinates and females that have just given birth may be vulnerable to social stresses. Extra care should be taken to prevent and monitor aggression and to separate individuals if necessary. Single housing for social species should only be considered on good husbandry or veterinary grounds. Objects can act as barriers within the pen and therefore allow animals greater control over their social interactions.

4. The needs of infants are different from those of adults. For example they may have differing space requirements from adult animals. An adequately complex social and physical environment during development is needed to produce normal adults.

Temperature

2.41. Animal room temperatures should be carefully controlled. Daily maximum/minimum temperatures should be recorded. The limits within which room temperatures should generally be maintained are detailed for each species. The equipment, insulation and design of the building should be such as to ensure that these temperatures can be maintained in both winter and summer.

2.42. The aim should be to maintain the animal room temperature within the range specified for the species. Fluctuations outside this range should be avoided.

2.43. It should be noted that temperatures within the cages will often be higher than room temperatures. Even in rat cages with grid floors in a room with adequate ventilation, the temperature can be 3–6°C above room temperature, according to the position of the cage in the room (15). The provision of bedding material allows the animal to manipulate its own immediate environment and provide a warm nest for its young.

2.44. Environmental controls should prevent undue fluctuations in temperature within or between rooms, thus avoiding unnecessary stress.

2.45. Outside exercise areas for dogs, cats and primates should provide shade during summer months, and access to shelter during inclement weather.

Relative Humidity

2.46. Extreme variations in relative humidity can adversely affect the well-being of some species (15), breeding performance (16) and, by affecting the rate of heat loss, can influence activity and food intake (17).

The relative humidity in animal rooms should normally be maintained at 55%± 15%. For some species extended periods below 40% or above 70% should be avoided.

Ventilation

2.47. The ventilation system should:

(i)   provide sufficient air of an appropriate quality.

(ii)   regulate within prescribed limits temperature and humidity;

(iii)   reduce the levels and spread of odours, noxious gases, dust and infectious agents;

2.48. The air flow rates required, will, to a great extent, be dependent on the species and stocking densities of animals, and on the type of animal accommodation e.g. single tier versus multi tier caging; wire mesh versus solid sides. Some form of mechanical ventilation will be necessary for the majority of housing systems, in order to ensure satisfactory levels of air movement and temperature control are maintained at all times.

2.49. As indicated above, the ventilation rate of the room will be related to stocking density and to the heat generated by animals and equipment in the room (thermal load). In order to maintain suitable air quality 15–20 changes of fresh or air conditioned air per hour distributed throughout the room would normally be adequate for rooms with high stocking densities eg rodents; rabbits. For cats, dogs and primates, 10–12 changes per hour may be sufficient. Fewer air changes may be acceptable where stocking densities are low.

2.50. The distribution system should deliver air as evenly as possible to each cage or animal whilst avoiding draughts (18). Careful attention should be given to air inlet and outlet positions to ensure good air circulation and avoidance of draughts and noise disturbance. Environmental conditions for both staff and animals will be improved by higher rates of air changes with a properly directed air flow.

Lighting

2.51. Adequate light should be available for staff to perform husbandry tasks safely, including observation of the animals. Prolonged exposure of animals to high intensity lighting should be avoided. In tier caged systems, a cover will generally be required above the top row of caging.

Defined photoperiods are often used. The importance of light to dark (L:D) cycles in regulating circadian rhythms and stimulating and synchronising breeding cycles is well documented (19). Where animals are maintained on reverse photoperiod, daily inspections of the animals must still be undertaken.

Noise

2.52. The control of noise is important in the care of laboratory animals (19, 20). Loud, unexpected and unfamiliar sounds including ultrasound can stress the animal, seriously disrupt breeding programmes and may cause behavioural disturbances (21). There is no indication that constant background noise, such as that generated by air-conditioning and similar equipment, is harmful to animals providing it is not too loud (22).

2.53. During the design of accommodation it is important that consideration is given to the use of materials and the siting of equipment which will minimise noise and vibration levels in the animal rooms. Equipment such as fire alarms, door bells and telephones should be of the so-called 'silent' type, which are inaudible to small rodents (23).

Emergency alarms and stand-by systems

2.54. An animal facility dependent upon technology is a vulnerable entity. It is strongly recommended that such facilities are appropriately protected to detect hazards such as fires and the breakdown of essential equipment such as ventilation fans, air heaters or coolers, and the intrusion of unauthorised persons.

2.55. Animal facilities which rely heavily on electrical or mechanical equipment for environmental control and protection will need a stand-by system to maintain essential services and emergency lighting systems as well as to ensure that alarm systems themselves do not fail to operate.

2.56. The heating and ventilation system should be equipped with monitoring devices or alarms to ensure that any faults can be quickly identified and promptly rectified.

3   ANIMAL CARE AND HEALTH

Introduction

3.1. Animals living within an animal house are totally dependent on humans for their health and well-being. The physical and psychological state of the animals will be influenced by their surroundings, food, water and the care and attention provided by the animal house staff.

3.2. The aim is to maintain animals in good health and physical condition; behaving normally for the species and strain, with a reasonable expression of their behavioural repertoire; amenable to handling; and suitable for the scientific procedures for which they are intended.

3.3. The general well-being of all animals must be checked at least once daily. Special care must be taken to ensure adequate monitoring of animals housed above head height and in the lower tiers of cage racks.

Responsibility for animals

3.4. Responsibility for the care of laboratory animals falls to:

(i)   the person undertaking daily care of the animals;

(ii) the person named as responsible for the day to day care of the animals;

(iii) the named veterinary surgeon who monitors and advises on the health and welfare of the animals;

(iv) the holder of the certificate of designation.

Sources of animals

3.5. Under section 10(3) of the Act, unless an exemption has been issued by the Secretary of State, the following species named in Schedule 2—mouse, rat, guinea-pig, hamster, rabbit, primate and quail (*Coturnix coturnix*) must be obtained from designated breeding or supplying establishments: dogs and cats must be bred at and obtained from designated breeding establishments.

3.6. The introduction of animals from non-designated sources either from within UK or from overseas will require the prior permission of the Secretary of State.

3.7. The importation of animals from overseas is controlled by the Animal Health Act 1981 and, for some species, by the Endangered Species (Import and Export) Act 1976. European Council Directive 92/65/EEC (BALAI Directive) states the requirements for the movement of some species of commercially traded laboratory animals within the Member States of the European Community. Details of licences, health certificates, rabies and other quarantine requirements should be obtained from the Animal Health Division, MAFF, or the Scottish Office Agriculture and Fisheries Department (SOAFD) and from the Wildlife and Conservation Licensing Section, Department of the Environment (DoE), Bristol. In Northern Ireland, importation is controlled by the Department of Agriculture.

Reception

3.8. New breeding or stock animals should be removed from their transport containers and examined by a responsible person with the least possible delay. The animals should then be transferred to clean cages or pens and be supplied with food and water as appropriate. Animals that are sick, injured or otherwise out of condition must be kept under close observation, housed separately and examined by a competent person as soon as possible and appropriate action taken.

3.9. A record should be made of animals received, their source and date of arrival as required by section 10(6)b of the Act. Animals should be identified by cage labelling in the case of rodents and other small laboratory animals. In the case of rabbits, dogs, cats and primates, each animal will need to be identifiable by a method of marking approved by the Secretary of State.

Despatch

3.10. Both consignor and recipient should agree the conditions of transport, departure and arrival times so that full preparation can be made for the animals' arrival, in order that they can be placed in previously prepared cages, fed, watered and rested.

Transport

3.11. Stress during transport should be minimised by making animals as comfortable as possible in their containers and, if confinement is to be prolonged, food and water must be provided. Time in transit should be kept to a minimum (24). Animals that are incompatible should not be transported together.

3.12. The number of animals within any one container must be such that animals travel in comfort with due regard to conditions likely to prevail throughout the journey.

3.13. The sender should ensure that the animals to be transported are in good health. Prior to packing each animal should be examined by an experienced, trained and responsible person. When animals are acquired from outside the UK, recipients should make it a condition of order that the above requirements are met. Sick or injured animals should be transported only for purposes of treatment or diagnosis.

3.14. Pregnant animals should not normally be transported in the last fifth of pregnancy.

Surgically prepared animals, neonates, nursing animals or animals with clinical genotypic defects may require additional care during transport.

3.15. The container should:

1. Confine the animals in comfortable hygienic conditions with minimal stress for the duration of the journey;

2. Contain sufficient food and water or moisture in a suitable form;

3. Contain sufficient bedding so that animals remain comfortable and in conditions close to their thermo-neutral zone;

4. Be of such a design and finish that an animal will not damage itself during loading, transport and whilst being removed from the container;

5. Be escape-proof, leak-proof and capable of being handled without the animals posing a risk to handlers;

6. Be designed to prevent or limit the entry of micro-organisms;

7. Be designed so that they can be thoroughly disinfected between shipments, if intended to be reusable;

8. Allow sufficient ventilation;

9. Be clearly labelled.

Containers holding animals should be moved carefully without rough handling, excessive noise or vibration.

3.16. Animals should be packed into containers as near as possible to the time of departure. Personnel responsible for the care and welfare of animals in transit must be aware of the needs of each species under their care. This applies to packers, cargo handlers, carrying agents and drivers of vehicles. Training and instruction should be reviewed regularly.

Useful additional information on aspects of transport may be found in the LABA/LASA guidelines for the care of laboratory animals in transit (25).

Transport of animals by air should comply with current IATA Guidelines (26).

All transport of laboratory animals within the United Kingdom must comply with the relevant transport of animals legislation (27).

3.17. In the case of animals carrying transgenes or harmful mutations or which are otherwise subject to control under the Act through their use in regulated procedures, it is necessary to consult the Inspector about authority to transfer them to other designated premises. Where laboratory animals are to be exported or imported advice should be sought from the Home Office and the local Divisional Veterinary Office of MAFF.

Acclimatisation and quarantine

3.18. Acclimatisation is necessary for an animal to overcome the stress imposed by transport and subsequent exposure to a new environment with different diet, microflora and a change of human contacts, before subjecting it to scientific procedures. The period of time required will vary according to circumstances and should be determined by the user in conjunction with the named day-to-day care person, a senior animal technician or named veterinary surgeon.

CARE OF ANIMALS

Animal accommodation

3.19. The caging or housing system is one of the most important elements in the physical and social environment of animals. It should be designed carefully to ensure animal well-being, particularly so when breeding animals may be maintained for considerable periods of time. The housing system should:—

1. Provide adequate space which permits freedom of movement and normal postural adjustment, and has a resting place appropriate to the species;

2. Provide a comfortable environment;

3. Provide an escape-proof enclosure that confines animals safely;

4. Provide easy access to food and water;

5. Provide adequate ventilation;

6. Meet the biological needs of the animals, e.g., maintenance of body temperature, urination, defecation, and, if appropriate, breeding;

7. Keep the animals dry and clean, consistent with species requirements;

8. Avoid unnecessary physical restraint.

3.20. Building and environmental control have been dealt with in Part 2. This section deals with the space required for each animal. Breeding establishments should always consult their Inspector before committing themselves to a programme of work to comply with the recommendations contained in this Code.

3.21. Size, shape and fittings of pens and cages should be designed, as far as is practicable, to meet the physiological and behavioural needs of the animals. The shape of the cage and the furniture provided can be as important to the animal as the overall size of the cage. Social relationships are as important as stocking densities and room must be allowed for growth of the animals. Some animals continue to grow into old age although they may become less active.

3.22. Cage and pen dimensions are given for each species in Part 2. The height and area recommended are the internal, not overall, dimensions. The sizes suggested are broadly in line with the recommendations of the European Convention (5) and of European Directive 86/609 EEC (4).

3.23. The sizes specified are minimum standards. Cages below the tabled heights and floor areas may be accepted temporarily at the discretion of the Home Office provided that the welfare of animals is not impaired. However, all new purpose-built housing should at least comply with the stated dimensions from the outset.

3.24. The pens or cages should be made of material that is not detrimental to the health of the animals and which is durable and will withstand normal cleaning techniques. They should be designed to minimise risk of injury with comfortable floors that permit easy removal of excreta. Floors, walls and doors should have surfaces which are resistant to wear and tear caused by the animals or by cleaning procedures.

3.25. Animals should be housed so that they can be inspected easily; animals must not be held in cages which are so high that they cannot be inspected without removing them from the rack.

3.26. Pens for larger animals should have stable, non-slip floors. If slatted floors are used, design and finish must allow the animals to lie comfortably without injury to legs or feet. A resting solid floored area should be provided.

3.27. Post-operative recovery and hospitalisation pens and cages may be smaller than the sizes suggested. Such housing should be used for the minimum time only, and only under the direction of the named veterinary surgeon.

Bedding and nesting material

3.28. Bedding and nesting material must be provided for breeding animals, unless it is clearly inappropriate to the species. It should be comfortable for the particular species, dry, absorbent, dust free, non-toxic and free from infectious agents, vermin and other forms of contamination. Sawdust or shavings should not be derived from hardwoods or wood that has been treated chemically. Nesting materials should provide insulation but cause no hazard to the young or adult animals (28). Nesting boxes and secure private areas in the pen or cage should be included as appropriate.

Food

3.29. Diet should be formulated to satisfy the nutritional requirements of the animals (29, 30, 31). In the selection, production and preparation of food, precautions should be taken to avoid chemical, physical and microbiological contamination. When appropriate, food should be packed in sealed bags that are stamped with the production date and, when applicable, the expiry date. Packing, transport and storage should be such as to avoid contamination, deterioration or destruction of food. Perishable foods should be stored in cold rooms, refrigerators or freezers.

3.30. All food hoppers and utensils should be cleaned regularly and preferably sterilised. If moist food is used or if the food is easily contaminated, daily cleaning is essential.

3.31. Where animals are held in groups, care should be taken to ensure that subordinate animals have adequate access to food and water. Consideration should be given to controlling food intake to avoid obesity in adult breeding stock.

Water

3.32. Clean drinking water must be available to all animals at all times. It is usually provided in water bottles or other containers or by an automatic system. During transport, it is acceptable in some cases to provide water in the form of a moist diet (25).

All bottles and accessories should be dismantled, cleaned and sterilised at intervals. Bottles should be replaced by clean, full ones rather than being topped up in the animal rooms. Water containers should not tip or spill easily.

3.33. The operation of automatic systems should be checked daily. Such systems must be properly serviced and cleaned regularly to avoid malfunction and the risk of spread of disease. If solid-bottomed cages are used, precautions should be taken to avoid flooding. Emergency supplies should be available in case pipes freeze or supplies fail.

Environmental Enrichment

3.34. All animals must be allowed adequate space to express a wide behavioural repertoire. Animals should be socially housed wherever possible with compatible individuals, and only single housed if there is good justification on veterinary, husbandry or welfare grounds.

3.35. Although basic cage or pen designs provide space and surfaces, adequate complexity within this space is necessary to allow the animal to carry out a range of normal behaviours. Restricted environments can lead to behavioural and physiological abnormalities (32,33). Providing animals with a degree of control over their immediate environment has been shown to reduce a variety of stress indicators in a range of species. The use of appropriate enrichment techniques extends the range of activities available to the animal.

Environmental enrichment in animal caging should be allowed for at the design stage. In traditional caging, enrichment through the provision of appropriate materials, as is already practised by many breeders, can be beneficial.

3.36. Enrichment can be of two major types:—

1. Physical
Providing structures or devices within the cage or pen can facilitate the animal's exploration and/or full utilisation of the cage. For example, if appropriate bedding material is provided, rodents make greater use of their cages and make nests. Primates can be fed in ways that stimulate the species' foraging behaviour and reduces stereotypies.

2. Social
Allowing animals opportunities to socialise with their own kind or with handlers can be beneficial.

3.37. Enrichment should be appropriate to the animal's needs. Those responsible for the care of animals should understand the natural behaviour and biology of the species, so that they can make sensible and informed choices on enrichment. For some species of animals there is substantial literature on this topic (e.g. USDA Publication on enrichment in primates) (34).

Handling

3.38. All staff should be sympathetic, gentle and firm when dealing with the animals. Where appropriate, time should be set aside for handling and grooming.

Cleaning

3.39. Regular cleaning and maintenance and a high standard of hygiene are essential for good husbandry. Routines should be established for cleaning, washing, decontaminating or sterilising cages and accessories.

Cages must be thoroughly cleaned and disinfected or sterilised before animals are introduced. This reduces the risk of disease transmission and reduces behavioural stress on the animal.

ANIMAL HEALTH

3.40. Healthy animals are a prerequisite both for good animal welfare and for good science. Intercurrent infection in the animal population may call into question the validity of information obtained from scientific procedures and make interpretation of results difficult or even impossible.

3.41. It is essential that, in consultation with the named veterinary surgeon or other suitably qualified person, plans should be prepared to maintain health and to deal with possible disease outbreaks. As poor breeding performance may be an indication of underlying disease, comprehensive breeding records shall be maintained and performance assessed on a regular basis. Effective breeding, health and disease recording systems should be maintained in formats agreed by the named veterinary surgeon and the Home Office Inspector, and these should be available for inspection. Records should include details of reproductive performance, arrivals, departures, treatments and deaths of animals.

3.42. Most laboratory species are purpose-bred and healthy animals of known microbiological status are supplied for experimental procedures. Wild caught animals may harbour pathogens transmissible to man and other species. A barrier system or strict quarantine management procedures should be adopted to help reduce risks where there is a risk of infectious disease.

3.43. A suitable microbiological surveillance programme should be maintained. The frequency and type of screening will depend on the species and status of the animals e.g. Conventional; Specific Pathogen Free.

Results of a surveillance programme provide reassurance to users on the quality of animals, and will allow scientists to choose the most appropriate animals for the study, thus reducing animal wastage.

Regular health screening to specified standards is a requirement of the Laboratory Animal Breeders Association Accreditation Scheme (LABAAS) (35). The Federation of European Laboratory Animal Science Associations (FELASA) has published a suggested health screening programme for laboratory animals (36).

Breeding Records

3.44. Records must be maintained of source, use, and final disposal of all animals bred, kept for breeding, or for subsequent supply for use in scientific procedures. Section 10(6)(b) of the Act requires that records are maintained. These are important for husbandry and planning purposes and as an indicator of the animals' well-being and welfare.

Breeding performance is a sensitive barometer of good husbandry and therefore of the welfare of the animals. The appearance of pathogenic organisms in the animal breeding area, loss of environmental control, a poor batch of diet, or even an unsympathetic or poorly trained animal technician can affect the performance of the breeding colony, leading to reduced fertility, an increase in pre and post weaning mortality and/or reduction in growth rates. These effects will often precede any obvious clinical signs of ill health.

3.45. Good records are required to detect any decline in performance at an early stage to allow remedial action to be introduced.

In breeding colonies data should be maintained on colony size, individual performance per breeding female (also in some cases of individual male), total output of the colony, litter size, number of litters in a given period, pre-weaning and post weaning mortality. The data should be averaged over appropriate periods so that any change in performance will be rapidly identified. Acceptable performance targets must be agreed with the named veterinary surgeon.

Part 2

INDIVIDUAL SPECIES REQUIREMENTS

4   MICE, RATS, HAMSTERS

Introduction

4.1. Laboratory rodents are highly adaptable animals, selected for important traits such as ability to breed in laboratory conditions and docility. However, they do retain many of the traits of their wild counterparts, for example, grooming, exploratory activity, searching for food, burrowing and gnawing, and housing systems should aim to encompass these behavioural needs.

Mouse

The laboratory mouse is derived from a largely nocturnal burrowing and climbing ancestor which favoured building nests for temperature regulation and reproduction. Mice do not readily cross open spaces, as confirmed by utilisation of cage space studies. Mice are capable of assuming a wide range of social organisations and intense territoriality may be seen in reproductively active males. Pregnant and lactating females may prove aggressive in nest defence. As mice, particularly albino strains, have poor sight they rely heavily on the sense of smell and create patterns of urine markings in their environment.

Rat

As the rat is a very much more social animal than the mouse disruption to social groups should be minimised. Young animals are very exploratory and interact to an enormous degree (37). Rats are excellent climbers, avoid open spaces, and use urine spotting as a territorial marker. The senses of smell and hearing are highly developed, and these animals are particularly sensitive to ultrasound. Daylight vision is poor, but dim-light vision is effective in some pigmented strains. Activity is higher during hours of darkness.

Hamster

This species is very different from the rat and the mouse. The female is larger and more aggressive than the male. During pregnancy and lactation the female can be intensely aggressive, and can inflict serious injury on her mate. Group housing may reduce aggressiveness in this species (38). Female hamsters often provide a latrine area within the cage, mark areas with secretions from a flank gland, and frequently selectively reduce the size of their own litter by cannibalism. Careful control of environmental features, and prevention of disruption during routine husbandry practices are of particular importance in this species.

THE ENVIRONMENT

4.2. Laboratory rodents are species which choose to manipulate their own microenvironments via activities such as huddling, nest building and tunnelling. In general, the rodent's ability to control temperature', humidity and lighting is more important to its welfare than specifying ambient conditions within the room. The microclimate within the cage is of most importance to the animal, and welfare seems facilitated when rodents are able to control this, for example by provision of bedding material.

Temperature

4.3. The optimal temperature band for mice, rats and hamsters is 19–23°C.

Temperatures within the cages will often be higher than room temperatures. Even with grid floors and adequate ventilation the cage temperatures may be 3–6°C above room temperature. The difference is likely to be greater in the solid-floored cages used for breeding.

Provision of bedding or nesting material allows the animal an opportunity to manipulate its own immediate environments, and provide a warm nest for its young. This may also promote greater utilisation of the available space.

Relative Humidity

4.4. Humidity control is an important consideration for laboratory rodents.

For rodents relative humidities in the range of 55%±15 are acceptable.

As low relative humidities may contribute to the development of ring-tail in rats, levels of less than 40% should be avoided.

Ventilation

4.5. Specific air change rates in the room are less important than ensuring that there is an efficient flow within the rooms to keep the level of ammonia within the animals' immediate environment at an acceptable level. Stocking densities, husbandry practices and cage types (for example, solid or grid bottom) will influence air flow patterns and the consequent ventilation rate required.

Lighting

4.6. Light levels within cages are more important to the welfare of breeding rats, mice and hamsters than the light level in the room. Lighting intensity should be that only which is required by husbandry practices or safety reasons.

More use should be made of subdued lighting (e.g. red lighting which rodents cannot detect). All racks (especially those that are relatively high) should have shaded tops to prevent animals in the top row being exposed to excessive light (which can cause retinal degeneration). The importance of light to dark cycles in regulating circadian rhythms and stimulating and synchronising breeding cycles is well documented. A daily cycle of 12:12 is usual.

Animals, especially when breeding, should be given the opportunity to withdraw to shaded areas within the cage, for example by provision of adequate nesting materials.

Noise

4.7. Sudden irregular noises create more disturbance in breeding rodents than continuous or predictable sounds.

As rodent neonates use ultrasound production to communicate distress, it is important that extraneous noise is minimised. Ultrasound from cleaning devices, pressure hoses, trolley wheels, vacuum cleaners, computer VDU's may result in abnormal behaviour and disturbed breeding cycles.

Noise cannot be eliminated from an animal unit but care should be taken to minimise the generation of sudden extraneous audible and ultrasound noise in the vicinity of animals.

ANIMAL CARE AND HEALTH

4.8. Unless there is good husbandry/veterinary justification for individual housing, animals should be maintained in sociable groups. These groups should remain stable. Frequent mixing of groups of breeding mice and hamsters is strongly discouraged as this can be a source of intense stressful conflict (39).

Bedding and Nesting Material

4.9. Nesting materials are crucial to breeding rats, mice and hamsters to enable them to engineer appropriate microenvironments that facilitate the successful rearing of young. The bedding is also an important material on which all three species lay down patterns of odour cues. These cues are important to the animal's sense of security.

Food and Water

4.10. Where large numbers of breeding or stock animals are maintained in a single cage or pen, it is important to ensure that there are sufficient feeding and watering stations to avoid undue competition.

Cleaning

4.11. Routine cleaning and maintenance, and a high standard of hygiene are essential for good husbandry.

There is, however, a real danger of over cleaning cages used by pregnant animals and females with litters. Such disturbances can result in mismothering or cannibalism.

Odour marking is an important activity in these rodent species, and cleaning disturbances will cause a degree of social disruption.

Decisions on frequency of cleaning should therefore be based on cage system, type of animal, stocking densities, and the ability of ventilation systems to maintain suitable air quality.

Partial cleaning, for example removal and replacement of soiled bedding permits some odour cues to remain in the cage and reduces the disturbance to the animals.

Animal Accommodation

4.12. Cage enrichment and social interaction are considered to be of more value to the animal than simple floor space allocation. Indeed large featureless cages can induce anxiety in rats (40).

Cage/Pen Dimensions and Stocking Densities

Minimum Floor Area Requirements for Breeders (including litters)

Mice	Minimum Floor Area cm^2	Minimum Cage Height (cm)
Monogamous Pair (Outbred/Inbred)	300	12
Trio (Inbred)	300	12

For each additional female plus litter an additional 180cm^2 should be added.

Rats	Minimum Floor Area cm^2	Minimum Cage Height (cm)
Mother and litter) Monogamous pair) and litter)	900	18
Hamsters Mother and litter) Monogamous pair) and litter)	650	15

A. Mice

Minimum Floor Space Allocation (cm²)

Weight	A. When housed in groups	B. When housed singly
<20g	30	200
21–25g	45	200
26–30g	60	200
>30g	100	200

Minimum floor space for one or more mice – 200cm²
Minimum cage height – 12 cm

B. Rats

Minimum Floor Space Allocation (cm²)

Weight	A. When housed in groups	B. When housed singly
<100g	75	500
101–150g	100	500
151–250g	150	500
251–350g	250	700
351–450g	300	700
451–550g	350	700
>550g	400	800

Minimum floor space for one or more rats – 500cm²
Minimum cage height – < 250g–18cm
                          > 250g–20cm

C. Hamsters

Minimum Floor Space Allocation (cm²)

Weight	A. When housed in groups	B. When housed singly
<60g	80	300
61–90g	100	300
91–120g	120	300
>120g	165	300

Minimum floor space for one or more hamsters – 300cm²
Minimum cage height – 15cm

Breeding

4.13. Rats, mice and hamsters must be bred on solid floors, and provided with suitable bedding material (e.g. shredded paper or wood chippings) from which a nest can be constructed. This is important in thermoregulation of the microenvironment, and keeps the young together for efficient lactation.

Disturbance to the animals should be minimised during late pregnancy and early lactation to reduce the risk of mismothering or cannibalism.

Environmental Enrichment

4.14. Many rodent species attempt to divide up their own cages into areas for feeding, resting, urination and food storage. These divisions may be based on odour marks rather than physical division but partial barriers may be beneficial. To increase environmental complexity the addition of some form of cage enrichment is strongly recommended. Corrugated devices or tubes are examples of devices which have been used successfully for rodents and these have the added benefit of increasing utilisable floor areas for the animals.

As these rodent species are generally social animals, disruption of established groups should be minimised as this can be very stressful.

Records

4.15. Regular monitoring of health and reproductive data is essential to ensure that problems are identified at an early stage, and corrective action implemented to minimise any potential adverse welfare effects on the animals. This form of monitoring and assessment is of particular importance in rodent units when very large numbers of animals are often maintained in a breeding colony.

5 RABBITS

Introduction

5.1. The welfare of rabbits can undoubtedly be enhanced by enriching their environment and maintaining high standards of housing and care. Comparative studies of domesticated rabbits living in groups in large enclosures have shown that they retain a wide behavioural repertoire, similar to their wild type ancestors. There is increasing evidence to show that rabbits denied such freedom can lose normal locomotor activity, and suffer skeletal abnormalities (41,42). For practical systems of husbandry rabbits have to be confined. However, all animals should be allowed adequate space to perform a wide behavioural repertoire. The rabbit is a naturally gregarious species so attention should be paid to their social wellbeing.

THE ENVIRONMENT

Temperature

5.2. The optimal temperature range for housing breeding rabbits is 15–24°C. Temperature regulation should ensure that there are no undue fluctuations which could cause unnecessary stress, or clinical welfare problems.

If welfare problems occur in the animals which can be attributed to a failure to maintain suitable temperatures, provision for heating and/or cooling will be required.

Relative Humidity

5.3. There are no special requirements for rabbits, and relative humidity levels should be as stated in Section 2.

Ventilation

5.4. To maintain suitable air quality, air flow rate requirements may differ depending on the type of accommodation, with tiered racks of cages likely to require higher rates than single tiered open mesh cages or floor pens.

As rabbits shed considerable amounts of hair, the extract ducts should be cleaned regularly to ensure continued efficiency of ventilation.

Lighting

5.5. Lighting should be such that animals may be easily inspected. In a tier racking system care should be taken to ensure that animals in the top tier are not exposed directly to high intensity lighting.

Noise

5.6. Rabbits are easily frightened by sudden unexpected loud noise and may injure themselves in panic. Some forms of low-level background noise in the animal room may be beneficial in reducing the impact of sudden loud noises. As rabbits are sensitive to ultrasound (43), care should be taken to minimise the generation of extraneous audible and ultrasound noise in the vicinity of the animals.

Animal Care and Health

Animal accommodation

5.7. Three types of housing systems are commonly used for breeding rabbits for subsequent use in scientific research, namely suspended, tiered cages; open wire mesh cages and floor pens.

With competent management and husbandry practices there are welfare benefits to be gained for animals housed in social groups in floor pen accommodation, where a wider behavioural and locomotor repertoire can be expressed (44). However information on the effects of pen housing on commercial rabbit breeding is at present limited and inconclusive.

Suspended mesh caging does offer advantages over conventional racked solid caging:- the animals have good visual field, and have some social contact with adjacent rabbits. Animals are more easily observed, but one disadvantage is the lack of concealment. A suspended wire cage system has the added benefit that good air quality and movement may be more easily maintained.

If solid sided cages are used, these should be positioned such that the animals have visual contact with other rabbits.

Minimum Requirements for Housing Rabbits in Breeding and Post-weaned Stock

Breeders Doe + Litter	Minimum Floor Area (cm^2)	Minimum Cage Height (cm)
Up to 3kg	4000	45
Over 3kg	6400	45

Group Housing	Minimum Floor Area (cm^2)	Minimum Cage Height (cm)
up to 2.0kg	1500	40
up to 2.5kg	2000	45
up to 3.0kg	2500	45
up to 3.5kg	3000	45
up to 4.0kg	4000	45
up to 6.0kg	5400	45
over 6.0kg	6000	45

Single Housed (Stock)	Minimum Floor Area (cm^2)	Minimum Cage Height (cm)
up to 2kg	2000	40
up to 3kg	3000	45
up to 4kg	4000	45
up to 6kg	5400	45
over 6kg	6000	45

Environmental Enrichment

5.8. The welfare of rabbits housed in cages may be enhanced by environmental enrichment, for example the provision of hay, hay blocks or chew sticks.

Enrichment in floor pen systems is readily achieved by e.g. the incorporation of different compartments within a pen; use of boxes/pipes for concealment. The use of straw for bedding and hay in the diet provides additional environmental enrichment. Post-weaned animals should be maintained for as long as is possible in compatible groups.

Breeding

5.9. Nesting boxes must be provided for breeding does. Some substrate, for example hay or shredded paper, must be provided as bedding material. The box should be available for several days prior to littering to permit the doe to exhibit normal nesting behaviour.

The nesting area should be designed to contain the young rabbits in the early post-partum period, but be of sufficient size to permit suckling.

The young rabbits emerge from the nest-box at 2–3 weeks of age and are generally weaned at 4–6 weeks. Wherever possible litter-mates should be housed in groups post-weaning. This facilitates subsequent group housing programmes.

Does should be assessed for continued suitability for breeding before mating.

Records

5.10. If required it should be possible to trace a rabbit back from the User establishment to the Breeding establishment. It is necessary that each rabbit be individually identifiable.

6 GUINEA-PIGS

Introduction

6.1. Guinea pigs have relatively long gestation periods and the young are well developed at birth. The guinea pig may appear nervous but are tame and can be easily handled. They tend to "freeze" at unfamiliar sounds, and "stampede" as a group at a sudden unexpected movement. Male guinea pigs may fight, but aggression between sexes or amongst females is very uncommon (45, 46). As the guinea pig has a poorly developed capability for either jumping or climbing, this species may be held in a low walled open topped pen.

THE ENVIRONMENT

Temperature

6.2. Reproductive performance can be significantly impaired if good temperature control is not maintained.

The optimal temperature range for housing breeding guinea pigs is 15–24°C. Temperature regulation should prevent undue fluctuations to avoid causing unnecessary stress or clinical welfare problems.

If health or welfare problems occur in the animals which can be attributed to a failure to maintain suitable temperatures, provision for heating and/or cooling will be required.

Relative humidity

6.3. There are no special requirements for guinea pigs, and relative humidity levels should be as stated in Section 2.

Ventilation

6.4. To maintain suitable air quality, air flow rate requirements may differ dependent on the type of accommodation — floor pens; tiered racks; solid or mesh sides.

Lighting

6.5. Lighting should be such that animals may be easily inspected. In a tier racking system care should be taken to ensure that animals in the top tier are not exposed directly to high intensity lighting.

Noise

6.6. As guinea pigs are easily startled and may injure themselves in panic, care should be taken to minimise the generation of sudden extraneous audible and ultrasound noise in the vicinity of the animals.

ANIMAL CARE AND HEALTH

Animal accommodation

6.7. Solid-floored cages or pens or mesh floored cages are used to house breeding and stock guinea pigs.

Although mesh floored cages may offer some advantages over solid floor cages, for example to reduce disturbance during cleaning, and to eliminate cage flooding with automatic watering systems, it is essential that, where mesh floors are intended, a suitable mesh must be used to minimise the risk of injury to the animals' feet and legs. The mesh must be carefully inspected and well maintained to ensure that there are no loose or sharp projections. Faulty mesh floors can lead to serious injuries. In such an event, prompt action must be taken to correct the fault or replace the mesh floor with solid-bottomed cages or pens.

It is preferable that at least one side of the cage is mesh or transparent to give improved visual contact, and thus reduce disturbance to the animals.

A suitable substrate *must* be provided. Hay is frequently used for this purpose. In addition to the nutritional value to the animal, it provides a form of environmental enrichment. When hay is not used, reproductive performance may be reduced and an increase in stereotypic behaviour seen.

Minimum Requirements for Housing Guinea Pigs as Breeding and Post-weaned Stock		
Breeding	**Minimum Floor Area (cm^2)**	**Minimum Height (cm)**
Pair	1500	23
Individual Breeding		
Female in Harem	1000	23
Group Housing (Stock and Harems)	**Minimum Floor Area (cm^2)**	**Minimum Height (cm)**
up to 150g	200	20
up to 250g	300	20
up to 350g	400	20
up to 450g	500	23
up to 550g	600	23
> 550g	700	23

The minimum floor area for one or more guinea pigs is 700cm^2

Environmental enrichment

6.8. Guinea pigs are social animals and should therefore be maintained in groups or in breeding pairs. Single housing should only be used if there is good veterinary or husbandry justification.

Although nesting material is not an essential requirement for guinea pigs, some form of bedding material must be provided. The use of hay or a similar substrate will increase environmental complexity in a sterile cage environment, will encourage better utilisation of the available space, and will provide the opportunity for concealment. The addition of sterilised soft wood sticks for guinea pigs to gnaw may also be considered (47).

Diet

6.9. Guinea pigs are unable to synthesise Vitamin C (ascorbic acid] in sufficient quantity to meet their daily requirements. It is therefore essential that their diet is of suitable composition to meet this requirement.

Breeding

6.10. Guinea pigs are generally bred as breeding pairs or in harems. The offspring are fully developed at birth. Weaning takes place at 2–3 weeks, but generally the young are eating solid food and drinking water within a few days of birth.

Young animals must be maintained in compatible groups.

7 DOGS

Introduction

7.1. Social contact, canine and human, should be a priority in the housing and care of dogs. Prolonged single housing must be minimised, with additional daily human contact necessary when such housing is unavoidable. Staffing levels must be sufficient to permit socialisation and regular `human contact.

As well as being important for animal welfare, good social interactions promote production of well – conditioned animals of suitable temperament for subsequent studies.

THE ENVIRONMENT

Temperature

7.2. **Adults** – As dogs have wide thermoneutral zones this species can normally be held at **ambient** temperatures in the UK without adverse effect. Suitable contingency plans should be prepared to deal with extremes of temperature, seen occasionally in hot summers or cold winters, to ensure that a comfortable environment is maintained for the animals. A suitable temperature range for beagles is considered to be 15-24°C. Heating and/or cooling should be provided if animals are held indoors for prolonged periods outwith this range of temperature. Outdoor pens must provide shelter against adverse weather conditions.

New-born – Puppies require a local environmental temperature of 26–28°C for at least the first 5–10 days of life (48).

Relative Humidity

7.3. There are no reported adverse effects resulting from dogs exposed to wide fluctuations of **ambient** relative humidity. It is considered unnecessary to control or record relative humidity.

Ventilation

7.4. For dogs held at required stocking densities 10–12 air changes are suitable for all enclosed areas. Lower stocking densities may permit fewer air changes.

Lighting

7.5. Lighting intensity must be adequate to allow safe working and inspection of all animals.

The photoperiod should be not less than 12 hours light. Where natural lighting is excluded provision of low level night lighting may be of benefit to the dogs.

Noise

7.6. It is important to design kennelling using suitable sound absorbing materials commensurate with hygiene. Sound levels can be considerably reduced by appropriate engineering design.

ANIMAL CARE AND HEALTH

Animal accommodation

7.7. Dogs should be housed socially (except in the case of the periparturient bitch). It is particularly important that these animals receive adequate social contacts with other dogs and humans during the primary socialisation period (3–14 weeks). After weaning it is common practice to house them in same sex groups. Long term single housing and social isolation are closely associated with a range of behavioural disturbances (49, 50) and should only be used as an option of last resort for an aggressive dog, or as above in the case of the periparturient bitch. In these cases, additional daily human social contact is necessary. Housing should be secure and present the minimum hazard to the handler and to the animals. Within this constraint it should provide adequate space, environmental complexity, and opportunities for social interaction.

Veterinary hospitalisation and isolation facilities must be provided. Where such facilities are below the space requirements outlined in these Codes of Practice or limit social contact with other dogs, the amount of time spent in them by dogs needing treatment should be restricted to the minimum necessary and used only as directed by a veterinary surgeon.

Dog pens should be subdivided into a separate sleeping and exercise area (32). This provides some environmental complexity and allows the animal to defecate/urinate away from its sleeping area.

The following requirements refer to pen sizes for beagles of less than 25kg body weight. Where it is required to keep breeding colonies of breeds over 25kg bodyweight advice should be sought from the Home Office Inspectorate.

A. **BROOD STOCK AND STUD DOGS – minimum space requirements**
Brood bitches and stud dogs: $2.25m^2$/animal
Minimum pen height   : 2.0m.
No dog must be kept in a pen of less than $4.5m^2$.

B. **WHELPING BITCH AND LITTER TO 6 WEEKS**
The periparturient bitch should only be moved to the whelping area within two weeks of expected parturition and while in the whelping area should have additional daily human contact.

A suitable whelping box or bed together with bedding material must be provided for the whelping bitch. Attention is also drawn again to the requirement for a *local* environmental temperature of 26–28°C for at least the first 5–10 days of puppies' lives.

THE MINIMUM PEN SIZE FOR BITCH AND LITTER TO 6 WEEKS IS $4.5m^2$
Two adult beagles can be expected to share this amount of space for extended periods of time in a user establishment. Whilst beagle litters may range in

size from 1–10 puppies, the average litter size is usually 5–6 pups. Puppies will leave the nest rarely but will increasingly do so during the first 2 weeks of life. Thereafter they will begin to explore and play in the pen with close maternal supervision. It is considered more important and appropriate to remove the mother from the litter at around 6 weeks of age (weaning) when her maternal instincts begins to wane rather than provide additional space.

C. **POST WEANED STOCK**

The usable space available to individual animals is much greater where they are housed in large groups. This is the situation generally found in breeding establishments.

Minimum space requirements:–

Body Weight	Minimum Floor Space
> 2kg	0.5m^2
> 5kg	1.0m^2
>10kg	1.5m^2
>15kg	2.0m^2
>20kg	2.25m^2

The table above indicates the minimum floor space which must be continuously available to each dog of the weight indicated.
The minimum pen size is 4.5m^2.
The minimum pen height should be not less than 2m.

Cleaning

7.8. Animals should be **relocated** to a separate pen/or dry compartment during wet cleaning of pens and not be returned until the home pen is sufficiently dry.

Breeding

7.9. Individual bitches must only be allowed to continue breeding if their current health status and previous reproductive history has been assessed and found to be acceptable. Bitches in poor condition or with a record of poor productivity should not be returned to breeding. Older bitches in particular should be carefully monitored to ensure continued suitability for breeding.

Environmental Enrichment

7.10. The welfare of dogs can be enhanced by environmental and social enrichment (51). A balance of human and canine social contacts together with exposure to a degree of novelty during development helps to produce a relaxed and friendly dog (52). Socially housed dogs must be compatible. Dogs vary in temperament and sympathetic husbandry practices will take this into account. Pens should have sufficient depth to allow nervous dogs to retreat from the front of the pen.

Solid partitions between pens are necessary to prevent injuries and to provide some privacy. This is particularly important for the whelping bitch. However, dogs are by nature inquisitive about their surroundings, which can be catered for by lower solid partitions towards the front of the pen and by as wide a field of view as possible from the pens.

Given the opportunity, dogs make extensive use of chews, particularly if they are food flavoured. Such items can be suspended just off the ground to keep them clean and to avoid monopolisation by dominant animals (51).

Staffing

7.11. The number of staff must be adequate to maintain the size of breeding colony and good standards of husbandry and care. In setting staff levels it is most important to take into account the essential human social interactions required, especially of the pups and single housed animals.

8 CATS

Introduction

8.1. Cats are social animals and management practices should ensure regular contact with other cats and humans. As well as being important for animal welfare good social interactions encourage production of properly conditioned animals of suitable temperament for subsequent studies. Cats are excellent climbers and choose to spend much of their time on shelves raised from the floor. Pen design must take account of this strong behavioural instinct.

THE ENVIRONMENT

Temperature

8.2. As cats have wide thermoneutral zones, this species can normally be held at ambient temperatures in the UK without adverse effects. Suitable contingency plans should be prepared to deal with extremes of temperature seen occasionally during hot summers or cold winters, to ensure that cats are maintained in a comfortable environment.

The optimum temperature range is considered to be 15–24°C.

Heating and cooling will be required if animals are held indoors for prolonged periods outside of this temperature range. Outdoor pens must provide shelter against adverse weather conditions.

Relative Humidity

8.3. There are no reports of adverse effects resulting from cats being exposed to wide fluctuations of ambient relative humidity. It is considered unnecessary to control or record relative humidity.

Ventilation

8.4. For cats held at the required minimum stocking densities 10–12 air changes are suitable for all enclosed areas. Lower stocking densities may permit fewer air changes.

Lighting

8.5. Lighting intensity must be adequate to allow safe working and inspection of all animals. The photoperiod may be varied in cat colonies as a method of controlling the reproductive cycle. Normal photoperiod allows 14 hours of light, but this may be reduced to a minimum of 8 hours where control of the reproductive cycle is being undertaken.

Noise

8.6. As cats are sensitive and easily startled by sudden unexpected noises, background sound (such as radio music when played **quietly**) is considered advantageous as this accustoms them to sounds of strange voices and reduces the impact of sudden loud noises (28).

ANIMAL CARE AND HEALTH

Animal Accommodation

8.7. The cat should, normally, be housed socially (except the periparturient queen) and it is particularly important that it receives adequate social contacts with other cats and humans during the primary socialisation period (3–14 weeks). After weaning it is common practice to keep cats in same sex groups. Long term single housing and social isolation can lead to behavioural disturbances, and should only be used as a last resort for an aggressive cat or, as above, for the periparturient queen. In these cases additional daily human social contact is required. Suitable veterinary, hospitalisation and isolation facilities must be provided.

1. **PERIPARTURIENT QUEEN AND LITTER TO 3 WEEKS.**

    The pregnant queen should be housed singly only in late pregnancy, preferably within the last week. Periparturient queens seek isolation in a confined space for the act of parturition and for a time in the early stages of suckling their young. For this reason, it is advised that the queen be provided with a quiet private area. Where there is confinement within a cage environment, **additional exercise must be provided for the queen on a daily basis with access to human social contact and ancillary play equipment.**

    Queen and litter to 3 weeks of age – minimum space requirement – $1.00m^2$ of usable space. Minimum height of 80cm. A useable shelf or solid nest box lid should be supplied to permit the queen some personal space distant from the litter.

2. **QUEEN AND LITTER FROM 3 WEEKS OF AGE TO WEANING – MINIMUM SPACE REQUIREMENTS.**

    $0.5m^2$/queen with an additional $0.1m^2$ for each kitten in the litter.

    Minimum pen size for any holding of queens and litters from 3 weeks to weaning must be $2m^2$ and 2m high.

3. **POST WEANED STOCK AND ADULT MALE AND FEMALE BROOD STOCK – MINIMUM SPACE REQUIREMENTS.**

    Provision of space must be via pen housing with a minimum height of 2m.

Body Weight	Minimum Floor Space
<1kg	$0.2m^2$
<2kg	$0.35m^2$
<3kg	$0.5m^2$
>3kg	$0.75m^2$

    No animals must be kept in a pen of less than $1m^2$ and 2m high.

Environmental Enrichment

8.8. Cats should be housed in social groups.

Housing should provide a complex and stimulating environment (53). Pens should contain litter trays, ample useable shelf room for resting and objects suitable for climbing and claw trimming.

Staffing

8.9. Staff levels must be adequate for the size of breeding colony and husbandry practices followed. In setting staff levels it is most important to take into account time for the important human social interactions required, especially of the kittens and single housed animals. This must include regular animal handling.

9 NON-HUMAN PRIMATES

Introduction

9.1. The order Primata includes both human and non-human primates; the latter encompass a wide range of life styles and sizes from the 60g mouse lemur to the great apes. In considering the provision of a suitable breeding environment for such a widely diverse group, it is best to work from a thorough understanding of the biological needs of the individual species. Separate sections are presented detailing requirements for the commonly bred laboratory non-human primates. Where there is an intention to breed a species not included in this document, the Home Office will advise on a case by case basis, and such advice may be subsequently added as a supplement to this section.

Non-human primates are highly intelligent, most have arboreal habits, and all need a complex, stimulating environment. Housing should provide adequate space, complexity (e.g. varied diets; cage furniture) and opportunities for social interaction. Their use of space means that cage volume is important. Most show a vertical flight reaction when disturbed; cage heights should allow for this and should permit the animals to stand erect, jump and climb, and to sit on a perch without the head or tail touching the cage.

Acquisition of animals

9.2. Captive bred non-human primates should always be used in preference to wild caught individuals. Captive bred animals are of known age, parentage, health status and have been reared in a controlled environment with domesticated husbandry practices. In addition to the possible effects on conservation, concerns have been raised over the welfare of animals during trapping and the subsequent housing conditions in the country of origin prior to export.

The establishment of breeding colonies of non-human primates is thus strongly encouraged in order that the welfare and quality of the animals are improved, and the demand on wild animal populations will be eliminated.

Where non-human primates are to be imported for breeding, they should, whenever possible, be obtained as offspring from reputable established breeding colonies. Such colonies should have high standards of health care and management similar to those outlined in the Codes of Practice issued by the International Primate Society (IPS) International Guidelines for the Acquisition, Care and Breeding of Non-human Primates (54). Those responsible for importing such animals should be familiar with IPS guidelines and verify that they are being implemented in the establishments from which they obtain their stock. Transport of non-human primates must comply with the International Air Transport Association's Live Animals Regulations (26) including the design and construction of containers.

Additional useful information on transport of non-human primates is detailed in the LABA/LASA Guidelines for the care of laboratory animals in transit (25).

The use of wild caught non-human primates will only be permitted in exceptional circumstances where there is strong scientific justification.

RECEIPT AND DESPATCH OF ANIMALS

The undernoted principles apply to international transport and to transport within U.K..

Receipt

9.3. Animals must be removed from their transport containers soon after they arrive. Particular care should be taken during handling at this time to minimise the stress caused to the animals. After inspection they must be transferred to their home cages, where applicable in a suitable quarantine area, and be provided with food and water without delay. Where possible food of a type familiar to them should be offered, and new diets introduced gradually.

Sick or injured animals must receive prompt veterinary attention. Where animals have died during transit or soon after arrival a post-mortem examination should be performed to ascertain the cause of death. The supplier should be informed and action taken to minimise the risk of any recurrence. A record must be made of each individual animal received, including its source, date of arrival and health status. Where individual animal records are supplied, these should be matched to the appropriate animal. Wherever possible animals should be acquired/supplied with lifetime health records.

A period of acclimatisation is necessary to enable animals to recover from any transport stress, and to become accustomed to their new environment. The required acclimatisation period will vary with the species, the journey and the facilities available. Imported animals are subjected to other statutory controls issued by the Ministry of Agriculture, Fisheries and Food, which require a period of quarantine for non-human primates, and the Department of the Environment. The requirements of these Departments must be taken into account.

Despatch

9.4. Non-human primates fear strange environments encountered during transport. There are a number of basic principles which the carrier should follow in order to ensure the welfare and comfort of the animal, and which will influence the animal's behaviour during transport. Stress may cause the animal to become difficult to manage. It is natural for monkeys to investigate their surroundings and try to escape. With very few exceptions, monkeys do not willingly accept confinement, and will often make determined efforts to escape. Familiarisation with the transport box prior to travel can reduce stress in the animal. Transport containers must be of suitable design and construction to minimise risk of escape. Vehicles used for transport should have two sets of doors/gates into the animal compartment, with a viewing port in the inner door.

Transportation of monkeys suckling young should not normally be undertaken. Some females, sensing danger, may harm their young. However, if in exceptional circumstances nursing monkeys have to be transported, they should be carried together with their young, but separated from other members of the group. Juvenile monkeys should not be separated from one another as this increases stress. Ideally they should be transported in pre-established pairs; if this is not feasible they should be in partitioned containers or in separate containers loaded adjacent to each other.

Monkeys of the same species and sex may be transported together in the same container only if they have previously been shown to be compatible. Otherwise, they should be carried separately. Food and moisture must be provided. Water is then not usually required during the first 24 hours following packing, but it is recommended that a small quantity of fresh fruit or vegetables be put in the container during packing.

Most species can withstand reasonable variations in temperature but exposure to wind and cold can be fatal. Consideration therefore must be given not only to the temperature fluctuations but also to the chill factors involved. Monkeys should never be exposed to direct heat, for example, by placing them in direct sunlight or against hot radiators, from where they are unable to escape.

It is essential that the animals be in good health. A veterinary health inspection should be carried out not more than 48 hours prior to travel. Animals must be accompanied on the journey by an appropriate veterinary certificate of health. There are a number of infectious diseases communicable to man that are carried by monkeys. Consequently, care must be taken to minimise physical contact with the animal and full personal hygiene precautions should always be taken. All containers and vehicles should be cleaned and disinfected after the journey. All animal containers must be securely anchored and spaced to prevent injury from movement or from adjacent animals.

Animal identification

9.5. If not already suitably identified, each animal should be individually identified, as soon as possible after arrival, by a method of permanent marking agreed with the Home Office Inspector.

Young animals should be identified at an appropriate stage before or around weaning.

As permanent identification may not be practicable in some species e.g. Marmosets, these animals may be fitted with a numbered collar or necklace.

The introduction of microchip identification offers a minimally invasive alternative to the commonly practised tattooing method of identification.

As the majority of non-human primates requiring to be identified will be recent arrivals or young animals around weaning the animals should under normal circumstances be sedated for the purposes of tattooing, as this will reduce stress in the animals and reduce the risk of injury to the handler. However, there may be circumstances in which sedation may not be required e.g. a tractable, well-handled animal. Where there is any possibility that the animal's welfare could be improved, or the handler's health and safety better protected some form of sedation must be given for the purposes of tattooing.

Animal health

9.6. As a wide range of animal and human diseases may affect the different species of non-human primates, it is essential that in consultation with the named veterinary surgeon, plans be prepared to prevent or deal with possible disease outbreaks. Physical separation of animals by species is generally recommended to prevent inter-species disease transmission and to reduce the stress caused by inter-species conflict. New World, Old World African and Old World Asian non-human primates should be housed separately as latent infections in one group can cause serious clinical disease in others.

Animals which may harbour zoonotic agents should be housed, managed and handled in such a way as to minimise any risk of infections being transmitted. Elimination of zoonotic and other infectious agents should be a priority in a breeding unit. All animals should be observed daily for signs of illness and injury, and observed for psychological well-being by an experienced animal care person familiar with the species. Individual animals showing evidence of disease or injury which warrants isolation must be removed from the colony and given appropriate treatment.

An effective health monitoring system should be maintained and be available for inspection.

Breeding programmes

9.7. Breeding of primates for use in scientific procedures will only be permitted in those institutions with proper facilities and experienced personnel.

Single housing should be avoided unless there are good veterinary or husbandry reasons.

The main breeding systems commonly used are as follows:—

1. Polygamous groups

Groups are generally comprised of 1–2 males and 4–12 females. If one male is used, accurate paternal determination is possible but conception dates can be difficult to determine. Groups should be closely monitored to check whether any animal is being excessively harassed and that all animals have adequate access to food and water. The provision of environmental enrichment and visual barriers is important.

This system requires enclosures or large rooms rather than cages. Multiple food and water sites should be available. Advantages include more efficient utilisation of space, less labour, and the provision of continuous exercise and social interaction for the animals.

Disadvantages can include difficulties in identifying, monitoring and capturing animals, a higher risk of injuries and questionable or unknown parentage.

2. Family groups

Monogamous species (e.g. Marmosets) live in family groups in the wild.

It is essential that animals are not weaned until an appropriate age for the species. Early weaning should be avoided as it can have profound deleterious affects on adult behaviour.

Staff education and training

9.8. Training of animal care staff working in non-human primate units must be carried out by appropriately experienced and competent persons. The two major themes of animal welfare and staff health and safety should be emphasised. Caring for non-human primates must take account of the social and psychological needs of each relevant species. Some animals can be powerful and aggressive and may be carrying pathogenic, infectious micro-organisms. Operating procedures in the unit should, therefore, minimise hazards to staff by controlling infection and ensuring the security of the building.

Comprehensive training should be provided in the catching and handling of non-human primates in a safe and humane manner. Methods of restraint and humane killing methods must be explained and carried out by experienced competent staff only.

INDIVIDUAL SPECIES REQUIREMENTS

NEW WORLD MONKEYS *(Platyrrhini)*

9.9. The new world monkeys comprise two families, the *Callitrichidae* and *Cebidae*, the members of which vary greatly in form, size, dietary requirements and habits.

Three groups are regularly bred for use in laboratories:—

    1.   Marmosets and Tamarins (*Callithrix* and *Saguinus*)

    2.   Owl Monkey (*Aotus*)

    3.   Squirrel Monkeys (*Saimiri*)

MARMOSETS *(Callithrix)*

Introduction

9.10. Marmosets are highly arboreal and territorial and in the wild live in family groups of up to 15 individuals, including a single breeding pair, in an area defined by scent. Infants are born at approximately five month intervals throughout the year; females normally bear and rear twins, although in captivity, triplet births are as common. In captivity, breeding groups should normally consist of a compatible pair and up to three sets of offspring, where juveniles gain experience in looking after infants and assist the parents with carrying them. Stock animals should be kept in same sex groups with a sibling if possible. Unfamiliar same-sex individuals may be very aggressive, so care should be taken when housing in same-sex groups.

Environmental enrichment should take into account the arboreal nature of marmosets. Swings, branches and perches should be provided. Wooden cage furniture should be provided to allow the animals to gnaw, a natural component of gum seeking and scent marking behaviour. In the wild, marmosets feed on fruit, insects, gum exudates and nectar. In captivity, care should be taken to maintain variety in the foodstuffs available.

ENVIRONMENT

Temperature

9.11. Range 20–28°C. Wide fluctuations within this range should be avoided. If the marmosets have access to outdoor runs or cages, they must be provided with heated indoor quarters. Shade and shelter from rain should be provided in out-door runs.

Relative humidity

9.12. Marmosets tolerate a high level of relative humidity (>90%) in the wild. Low relative humidities should be avoided. The normal range of 55±15% relative humidity is satisfactory, but higher levels are acceptable.

Ventilation

9.13. 10–15 air changes per hour will normally be adequate for the stocking densities suggested. Fewer air changes may be acceptable where stocking densities are low. Draughts should be avoided.

Lighting

9.14. A photoperiod of not less than 12 hours light is recommended. The intensity should be sufficient to permit adequate observation of the animals.

Noise

9.15. Care should be taken to minimise the generation of extraneous audible and ultrasound noise in the vicinity of the animals.

ANIMAL CARE AND HEALTH

Diet

9.16. A diet should be offered which provides all nutritional requirements. All species of New World Monkeys should be provided with diets containing adequate quantities of vitamin D3. The diet should be varied to reduce boredom.

Cleaning

9.17. The aim should be to achieve a satisfactory balance between the normal behavioural repertoire of the marmosets and good housekeeping. Care must be taken not to over clean fixtures and fittings as marking sites may be disrupted. Fixtures and fittings should be removed in rotation to ensure continuity of scent markings.

Animal accommodation

9.18. Marmosets have a large and varied behavioural repertoire, and housing should accommodate as far as is possible their behavioural needs, for example, sleeping and resting areas, social activities e.g. grooming; playing; breeding and communications, both visual and vocal.

Cages should be of a height to allow the marmosets to be at or above the height of the average technician. This provides an additional sense of security for the animals.

A complex and unpredictable cage environment is therefore necessary to permit effective locomotory, foraging and social skills, which also promote both physical and psychological well being. Places to hide or retreat from more dominant members are necessary.

Breeding programmmes

9.19. Established breeding pairs usually remain monogamous for the duration of their breeding life. It is important that prospective replacement breeding stock should have some experience of carrying babies before mating. This is generally achieved by keeping offspring within the group until after the birth of two further litters.

In breeding establishments two systems are commonly used:—

    (i)   Alpha pair whose offspring are supplied for use

    (ii)   Alpha pair plus offspring who are maintained in family groups until paired to form new breeding stock, or supplied for use.

Young animals for issue must not be separated from the breeding group until a minimum of six months old, preferably eight months, unless there are good veterinary or husbandry reasons for weaning earlier (e.g. hand reared triplets).

Animals to be used as future breeding stock should not be weaned until a minimum of thirteen months of age.

As considerable fighting can take place, newly constituted groups of animals should be monitored closely until these groups are well established.

Cage dimensions

9.20. The volume of usable space within the cage is more important for these arboreal animals than the linear dimensions of the cage.

GUIDELINES FOR HOUSING BREEDING GROUPS.

MARMOSETS

Minimum cage height

150 cm (Top of cage must be a minimum 180cm from floor).

Minimum floor area

    1.   Breeding Pair plus one generation of offspring — $0.55m^2$

    2.   Family group (8 Animals Maximum) — $1.0m^2$. This excludes carried infants.

    3.   Stock Animals — Minimum Pen Size — $0.55m^2$
                                    — Minimum floor area/animal — $0.135m^2$

Cage floors may either be solid or mesh with a catching tray underneath. If solid floors are provided they must be covered to a suitable depth with either sawdust, woodshavings or similar material.

Provision for foraging within a suitable substrate must be provided irrespective of floor type.

Environmental enrichment

9.21. The environment can be made more interesting by thoughtful utilisation of the space provided. Shelving should be strategically placed to increase the sense of security. Numerous feeding sites should be available. The inclusions of forage boxes, 'treat' boxes or artificial gum trees are useful. A safe retreat must be provided and many animals will use this for sleeping. Wooden nest boxes are preferred, although plastic containers have also been successfully used.

Activity will to a large extent depend on the quality of environment provided. A mixture of fixed and mobile fittings such as swinging platforms, plastic tubing, flexible tubing or wooden ladders and frames should be provided. Inclusion of natural branches has been found to be useful.

TAMARINS *(Saguinus)*

9.22. Tamarins are similar in most respects to marmosets, but there are some differences. They are larger animals and some are much more excitable than marmosets. Some species are seasonal breeders (*S. oedipus*). In the wild they range far more widely than marmosets and should be provided with more space in captivity. Their diet is similar to marmosets but they do not gouge for gum exudates.

9.23. GUIDELINES FOR HOUSING BREEDING GROUPS OF TAMARINS

Minimum cage sizes

Minimum Height	— 150cm usable height (Minimum — 180cm from floor)
Minimum Floor Area	— 1.5m^2 for family group
	— 0.15m^2/animal post weaning stock or adults
	— Minimum Floor Area 1.5m^2

OWL MONKEY *(Aotus)*

9.24. Owl monkeys are nocturnal animals, whose diet is predominantly fruit, but may include small birds, mammals and insects.

The animal is monogamous, and territorial.

As scent marking is important to this species, over cleaning should be avoided.

Owl monkeys may be held in similar conditions to those for tamarins and marmosets.

Lighting

9.25. The Owl Monkey is nocturnal and may be maintained under a 12:12 light: dark cycle or under natural lighting. Red lighting should be provided when full lighting is not required.

9.26. GUIDELINES FOR HOUSING BREEDING GROUPS OF OWL MONKEYS

Minimum cage sizes

Minimum Height	— 150cm usable height (Minimum — 180cm from floor)
Minimum Floor Area	— 1.5m^2 for family group (Max 5)
	— 0.135m^2 per stock animal less than 700g
	— 0.2m^2 per stock animal more than 700g
	— Minimum floor area — 1.5m^2

D. SQUIRREL MONKEYS *(Saimiri)*

9.27. This species is highly arboreal and polygamous. In the wild, males and females live in separate troops making prolonged contact only during the breeding season. Squirrel monkeys prefer to live with members of their own sex, so that weaned individuals can be kept in same sex groups without difficulty. In captivity breeding groups should consist of a minimum of three females, as smaller numbers do not show regular reproductive cycling. As the females dominate males, there should be at least two males in the breeding group and the cage should be divided in such a way as to allow the males to rest out of sight of the females. Thus a minimum-sized efficient breeding group will consist of 2 males and 3 females, but breeding groups may contain up to 8 females. Facilities should be provided for females giving birth to withdraw from the rest of the group. Sub-adult young can be removed from the parental group when 9-10 months old and kept in same-sex groups. Environmental enrichment should take into account the arboreal nature of the squirrel monkey and swings, branches and perches should be provided.

Diet

9.28. Squirrel monkeys forage mainly for arthropods in the wild supplementing them with fruit and flowers when they are less abundant. In captivity, they require a diet with high animal protein content, so that standard monkey diets are generally inadequate in this respect and require supplementation. They can be provided with arthropods (for example crickets or mealworms), egg or cheese, and they also should be given citrus fruit.

9.29. GUIDELINES FOR HOUSING BREEDING GROUPS OF SQUIRREL MONKEYS

Group	No of adult animals	Maximum number in cage	Cage floor area (m^2)
Breeding	5 (2m+3f)	8	2.0
	10 (4m+6f)	18	4.0
Weaned Animals	<700g	–	0.135
	>700g		0.2

Minimum cage floor area — 2.0m^2
Minimum cage height — 1.8m

2. OLD WORLD MONKEYS *(Cercopithecidae)*

Introduction

9.30. Amongst the old world monkeys are the macaques from Asia and North Africa and the baboons from Africa and South West Asia.

MACAQUES *(Macaca)*

The three species which are most commonly kept in laboratories are all from Asia:— *Macaca mulatta* (the rhesus monkey), *Macaca fascicularis* (the long-tailed, crab-eating or cynomolgus macaque) and *Macaca arctoides* (the stump-tailed macaque). In the wild, all live in matriarchal groups which include several adult males who have emigrated from other groups. There are both male and female dominance hierarchies and females form kinship groups within the troop. Social bonds are strongest between related females and males compete for access to females in oestrus. Two species, the rhesus monkey and stump tailed macaque live in warm to temperate climates, while the long-tailed macaque is a tropical species which particularly favours mangrove swamps and often forages in water. The long-tailed macaque is the most arboreal of the three species and the stump-tailed the most terrestrial. Rhesus and stump-tailed macaques are seasonal breeders while cynomolgus breeds all year round.

BABOONS *(Papio)*

Although baboons are not often bred in the laboratory, they are occasionally supplied for use in procedures. They live in a wide range of African habitats ranging from semi-desert to tropical rain forest. Baboons kept in laboratories generally belong to the *cynocephalus* group of species. In the wild they live in large multi-male multi-female groups basically similar in social organisation to macaques. Baboons are highly terrestrial but seek refuge and sleep in trees or on cliffs. They breed all the year round but may show a reproductive peak at a particular time of year. Baboons are highly intelligent and can easily be trained to cooperate with staff.

THE ENVIRONMENT

Temperature

9.31. Old world primates range from warm temperate to tropical climates, with wide variations of temperature experienced. A suitable temperature range for old world monkeys housed indoors is 15-24°C. As the tropical cynomolgus will require higher minimum temperatures than the sub-tropical to warm temperate Rhesus, care must be taken to ensure a comfortable environment is maintained when temperatures outwith this optimal range are experienced. In exclusively indoor accommodation temperatures can be maintained in the range 15–24°C, normally 19–23°C for staff comfort.

If the animals have outdoor runs or cages, they must have free access to heated indoor quarters with ambient temperatures as specified above. Shade and shelter from adverse weather conditions should be provided in outdoor runs.

Relative humidity

9.32. Old world primates occupy habitats which range from semi-desert (baboons) to lush tropical forest (some macaques). The animals adapt well, and the relative humidity in animal units of 55 ± 15% is satisfactory.

Ventilation

9.33. The rate of ventilation required will be related to stocking density, but 10–12 air changes per hour should be adequate.

Draughts should be avoided particularly when the animals are young.

Animal Care and Health

Diet

9.34. A diet should be offered which provides all nutritional requirements, supplemented daily by fresh fruit and/or vegetables.

A forage mixture should be scattered on the pen floor daily.

Cleaning

9.35. A system of cleaning should be adopted which minimises behavioural/social disruption. Pens may be part-cleaned in rotation e.g. outside and inside areas on separate days.

Breeding colonies

9.36. Macaques must be bred in groups.

For female bonded species (e.g. macaques) groups of females can easily be socially housed. Similarly, groups of males can be kept in single sex groups if introduced at an early age. However, pairs or groups of male macaques should not be kept in the vicinity of females as this may provoke male-male aggression.

Breeding groups will not normally contain fewer than six females and one male, although the recommended ratio is 12 females to one male. The maximum group size will be based upon the space available.

Future breeding groups should be made up at an age that causes least stress to the animal i.e. before sexual maturity. Once a breeding group is established it is not advised that additions be made, as this may cause considerable social disruption. Young animals must not be weaned at less than six months of age and 1kg in body weight, unless on veterinary advice e.g. mother is unable to rear baby. It is preferable not to wean before 12 months of age. Separation of animals pre-weaning for husbandry purposes should be avoided as this may result in maternal rejection.

Housing

9.37. Groups of macaques breed well in extensive pen systems. The pens must be designed to produce a complex environment suitable for these highly intelligent animals. For example, pens may contain shelves, swings, perches, climbing frames, hide/escape areas.

Where possible, pens should be designed to allow visual contact with other groups. Direct contact may provoke intergroup fighting and possible injury.

Multiple feeding and watering stations are required in large pens to prevent undue competition.

Outdoor pens should provide shelter from adverse weather conditions.

Provision should be made for capturing animals when required for veterinary or husbandry reasons.

As these animals spend considerable periods on the ground, the use of solid floored pens is recommended. Where grid floors are used, the animals must have access to a suitable solid resting and foraging area.

GUIDELINES FOR HOUSING BREEDING GROUPS OF MACAQUES

Minimum heights of pen or cages

Indoor   Outdoor
1.80m   2.4m

Pen sizes and stocking densities

The minimum pen sizes for any breeding group of macaques will be 6m².

a. *Macaca fascicularis* (Cynomolgus, long-tailed or crab-eating macaque)

— Approximate Weight Range of adults 4–10 kg.

In a breeding troop each adult will be provided with a minimum floor space of 1.0m². This area will include space for young animals up to 6 months of age.

For growing animals — 6 month — 1 year — 0.35m²
                      1 year   — 2 years — 0.45m²

The minimum pen size for a single replacement breeding or stock animal will be 2m².

b. *Macaca mulatta* (Rhesus)
  ***Macaca arctoides* (Stump-tailed macaque)**

— Approximate weight range of adults — 6–14kg.

In a breeding troop each adult will be provided with a minimum floor space of 1.7m². This area will include space for young animals up to 6 months of age.

For growing animals — 6 month — 1 year — 0.45m²
                      1 year   — 2 years — 0.6m²

The minimum pen size for a single replacement breeding or stock animal will be 2m².

3. OTHER SPECIES OF OLD WORLD MONKEYS

9.38. For other species of Old World non-human primates (e.g. *Papio*) held as stock animals in supplying establishments it is recommended that these animals be group-housed.

Primates imported for subsequent use in scientific procedures, and acclimatised or held at designated supplier establishments should be housed and caged in standards at least equivalent to those set out in the Code of Practice for the Housing and Care of Animals Used in Scientific Procedures (1).

Further guidance will be prepared by the Home Office if there is an intention to breed additional species to those detailed in section 9 of the present Code. Such information may be included in any future revision of this Code of Practice.

10 QUAIL — *Coturnix coturnix*

Introduction

10.1. Quail have been widely used in many areas of biomedical and behavioural research. Many of the welfare problems associated with the housing, care and husbandry of domestic poultry also apply to quail.

They are suited to reproduction and embryological studies due to their high egg production and rapid maturation rate (55).

THE ENVIRONMENT

Temperature

10.2. *Adults* – Breeding quail and mature stock birds should be maintained within the temperature range 16–23°C.

At low temperatures (<15°C) the males may become inactive and fertility severely affected (56).

Brooding and Growing Stock – The critical temperature for hatched chicks is 35–37°C. This temperature should be gradually reduced (approximately ½°C per day) to within the acceptable temperature range for the species (16–23°C) at four weeks of age.

Temperatures should be uniform within the breeding area.

Relative Humidity

10.3. Quail can be maintained within a wide range of Relative Humidity (30–80%) (57).

Ventilation

10.4. Good ventilation is essential to provide the birds with a constant and uniform supply of fresh air, and to extract from the building the products of respiration and the moisture and gases arising from the bedding and droppings. Ventilation rates will largely depend on stocking densities. Draughts at floor level should be avoided particularly in brooders.

Lighting

10.5. Lighting regimes will vary depending on the purpose for which the birds are intended. These are normally in the range of 16–24 hours of light per day, although stock birds are often maintained in a 8:16 light/dark cycle to slow down growth rates.

Lighting should be available for newly hatched chicks for 23 hours/day, gradually being reduced to 14 hours at 2 weeks.

ANIMAL CARE AND HEALTH

Animal accommodation

10.6. *Floor Pens* – Floor pens provide the birds with a greater freedom of movement, and the opportunity for wider social interaction. Less stereotypic behaviour is seen in floor pens than in cages.

Improved environments can be provided by the inclusion of dust baths, and artificial brush cover. However, as quail do not lay eggs in nests, significant numbers may be lost or damaged.

Quail have a very characteristic escape response which consists of a sudden vertical flight movement. As this can result in head damage if pens are too high, the tops of pens should be of a material which will not cause injury if the birds fly into it. eg loose netting (small mesh) or foam padding. A suggested maximum safe height is 60cm.

10.7. *Cages* – Cage systems offer a number of advantages over pens:– egg collection can be maximised; egg production can be easily monitored; fighting is minimised in established groups and less cranial trauma is seen (in suitably designed cages).

The major disadvantages are that space is restricted, stereotypic behaviour is common, and foot problems are frequently encountered.

Wire cages should be coated in plastic or similar material as this will be a factor in reducing head injuries and foot problems.

Minimum Space Requirements		
Minimum Floor Space Allocation (cm^2)		
Weight	A. When housed in groups	B. When housed singly
<75g	100	350
75–100g	150	350
100–150g	250	350
150–250g	250	400

Optimal cage height — **20cm**
Minimum length of trough per bird — **4cm**

Breeding Systems

10.8. In cage systems trios (2f + 1m) are often established at 3–4 weeks of age. Establishment of mating groups before sexual maturity (8 weeks) will reduce the incidence of aggression and feather pecking. Small group sizes seem to be more important than stocking densities in reducing mortality rates (58). Ratios of 1m to 2 or 3f are most commonly used. The mating behaviour of the male quail can be brutal, and unrelated to the receptivity of the female (58). Careful monitoring of mixed groups is necessary to monitor for damage as a result of repeated mating or feather pecking.

Female single sex groups can be satisfactorily maintained, but fighting is a serious problem in male groups.

Fertility and egg hatchability are optimal between 8–26 weeks of age, and tend to drop off rapidly after this time.

Egg production is variable between strains, with an average 70–90 eggs laid per bird per 100 days.

Incubation

10.9. Special care must be taken in the collection and handling of quail eggs as they are thin shelled and break easily. Hatchability is affected by the length of storage prior to incubation, and by the age of the parent stock. Although 80–90% hatchability is attainable, 50–60% is considered satisfactory. Storage of eggs post-collection at 13–15°C for a period not exceeding 7 days will give optimal hatchability. Extended pre-incubation storage should be avoided as this increases the incidence of abnormalities (59).

Quail eggs can be incubated in commercial incubators with wire mesh settings, or setting trays in which mesh can be fitted. The incubation for quail eggs is 16–18 days.

Hatching should be carried out in the hatching compartment of combined setter hatches or in small observation incubators.

Welfare Issues

10.10. Agonistic behaviour and damage to the female by an aggressive male can be minimised by careful grouping and monitoring of the birds.

Significant losses can occur due to head injuries caused by the birds striking the roof of the cage or pen. This is as a result of the quail's vertical flight response. Damage to the birds can be minimised by good pen or cage design.

Care should be taken with the composition and quantity of diet offered to the birds as skeletal and cardio pulmonary problems are frequently found in old caged birds.

Cage or pen floors should be designed to minimise foot contact with waste food or faeces as these can adhere to the feet causing discomfort to the birds.

Record Keeping

10.11. Records should be maintained of all birds produced for use in scientific procedures.

The minimum record keeping requirements for quail are detailed below:–

    a.   Number of breeding males and females.

    b.   Number of mature stock birds.

    c.   Numbers of eggs produced/collected.

    d.   Number of eggs incubated.

    e.   Number of eggs hatched.

    f.   Number of chicks reared in brooders (hatch – 4 weeks).

    g.   Health records – in consultation with Named Veterinary Surgeon.

    h.   Deaths.

11 BIBLIOGRAPHY

1. Home Office (1989) Code of Practice for the Housing and Care of Animals used in Scientific Procedures. London: HMSO

2. Royal Society/UFAW Guidelines on the Care of Laboratory Animals and their Use for Scientific Purposes: I – Housing and Care (1987) London: The Royal Society and the Universities Federation for Animal Welfare.

3. Laboratory Animals Breeders Association (LABA) Guidelines on the Care and Housing of Animals Bred for Scientific Purposes.

4. European Community 1986 Council Directive 86/609/EEC on the approximation of laws, regulations and administrative provisions of Member States regarding the protection of animals used for experimental and other scientific purposes. OJ L.358

5. Council of Europe (1986) European Convention for the Protection of Vertebrate Animals used for Experimental and other Scientific Purposes. Strasbourg: Council of Europe. (Obtainable: HMSO).

6. LASA recommendations on education and training for licence holders under the UK Animals (Scientific Procedures) Act 1986 – FELASA – FELASA Categories B and C Laboratory Animals (1993) 27, 189–205.

7. Categorisation of pathogens according to hazard and categories of containment (second edition 1990) London: HMSO.

8. Smith M. W. (1987) Safety. In the UFAW Handbook on the Care and Management of Laboratory Animals. 6th ed. ch.ll. pp 170–186 Harlow: Longman Group UK Ltd.

9. Health and Safety in animal facilities. Education Services Advisory Committee London: HMSO.

10. What you should know about allergy to laboratory animals. Education Services Advisory Committee London: HMSO.

11. RENTOKIL. Pest Exclusion. East Grinstead: Rentokil.

12. Waste Management, the Duty of Care, a Code of Practice 1991 HMSO: London

13. Institute of Animal Technology The Principles of Animal Technology 1 Editors Kelly P.J.; Millican K.G.; Organ P.J.

14. RCVS Code of Practice for Named Veterinary Surgeons employed in Scientific Procedure Establishments and Breeding and Supplying Establishments under the Animals (Scientific Procedures) Act 1986. 1992 Royal College of Veterinary Surgeons; London.

15. Clough, G. (1984) Environmental factors in relation to the comfort and well-being of Laboratory Animal Management. pp 7–24 Proceedings of a LASA/UFAW Symposium. Potters Bar: UFAW.

16. Donnelly, H. (1988) Effects of Humidity on Breeding Success in Laboratory Mice. In Laboratory Animal Welfare Research. pp 17–23. Proceedings of UFAW Symposium. Potters Bar: UFAW.

17. Stille, G., Brenzowsky, H., and Weike, W.H. (1968) The Influence of the Weather on the Locomotor Activity of Mice. Arzneimittel-Forschung 18: 892–893.

18. Clough, G., (1987) The Animal House: Design, Equipment and Environmental Control. In the UFAW Handbook on the Care and Management of Laboratory Animals (Ed. T.B. Poole): 6th ed., ch.8. pp 108–143, Harlow: Longman Group UK Ltd.

19. Clough, G., (1982) Environmental Effects of Animals Used in Biomedical Research. Biol.Rev. 57: 487–523.

20. Gamble, M.R., (1982) Sound and its Significance for Laboratory Animals. Biol.Rev. 57: 395–421.

21. Sales, G., Evans, J., Milligan, S., Langridge, A., (1988). Effects of Environmental Ultrasound on Behaviour of Laboratory Rats. In Laboratory Animal Welfare Research. pp 17–23. Proceedings of UFAW Symposium. Potters Bar: UFAW.

22. Pfaff, J. and Steckler, M., (1976) Loudness levels and Frequency Content of Noise in the Animal House. Lab. Anim. 10: 111–117.

23. Clough, G. and Fasham, J.A.L. (1975) A "silent" Fire Alarm. Lab. Anim. 9: 193–196.

24. Clough, G. and Townsend, G.H. (1987) Transport. In the UFAW Handbook on the Care and Management of Laboratory Animals: 6th Ed. ch. 10, pp 159–169. Harlow: Longman Group UK Ltd.

25. Guidelines for the Care of Laboratory Animals in transit – Laboratory Animals Breeders Association of Great Britain Limited and Laboratory Animal Science Association. (1993) Laboratory Animals 27, 93–107.

26. Live Animal Regulation 19th Edition International Air Transport Association Montreal: Geneva. Published annually.

27. Welfare of Animals during Transport Order 1992. HMSO: London.

28. UFAW (1987) The UFAW Handbook on the Care and Management of Laboratory Animals (Ed. T.B. Poole) 6th ed. Harlow: Longman Group, U.K. Ltd.

29. Nutrient Requirements of Domestic Animals No. 10 Nutrient Requirements of Laboratory Animals 3rd Revised Edition (1978) National Academy of Science, Washington DC.

30. Principles of LaboratoryAnimal Science (1993) Editors Van Zutphen, L.F.M. Baumens, V., Beynen, A.C., Amsterdam Elsevier: ISBN 0-444-81487-6.

31. Clarke, H.E., Coates, M.E., Eva, J.K., Ford, D.J., Milner, C.K., O'Donoghue P.N, Scott, P.P., and Ward, R.J., (1977) Dietary Standards for Laboratory

Animals: Report of the LAC Diets Advisory Committee. Lab.Anim. Volume 11 pps 1–28.

32. Fox, M.W., (1986) Laboratory Animal Husbandry: Ethology, Welfare and Experimental Variables., Albany: State University of New York Press.

33. Mason, G.S. (1991). Stereotypies: a critical review. Anim. Behav., 41: 1015–1037.

34. USDA/NIH/Primate Information Center, University of Washington 1992 Environmental Enrichment Information Resources for Nonhuman Primates: 1987–1992 (1992) It is available from the Animal Welfare Information Center (AWIC) of the USDA National Agricultural Library.

35. Laboratory Animal Breeders Association (1993) Accreditation Scheme 5th Edition.

36. Recommendations for the Health Monitoring of Mouse, Rat, Hamster, Guinea Pig and Rabbit Breeding Colonies, FELASA Working Group on Animal Health. (1994) Laboratory Animals 28, 1200–1212.

37. Poole, T.B., and Fish, J., (1976). An investigation of individual, age and sexual differences in the play of *Rattus Norvegicus* (Mammalia, Rodenta). Journal Zoology (London) 179: 249–260.

38. Brain, P.F., (1972). Effects of isolation/grouping on endocrine function and fighting behaviour in male and female Golden hamsters (*Mesocricetus auratus*), Waterhouse,) Behavioral Biology 7: 349–357.

39. Brain, P.F., (1990). Stress in agonistic contexts in rodents pp 73–85 In: Stress in Domestic Animals, R. Dantzer and R. Zayan (Eds), Dordrecht: Kluwer Academic Publishers.

40. Brain, P.F., Nastiti Kusumorini and Benton, D., (1991). 'Anxiety' in laboratory rodents: a brief review of some recent behavioural developments. Behavioural Processes 25: 71–80.

41. Stauffacher, M., (1991). Animal welfare in rabbit breeding; a housing system for breeding groups and an enriched cage. Paper presented to Joint RSPCA/FRAME/UFAW/BVA Workshop on Refinement of Rabbit Housing, London, 12 November 1991.

42. Rothfritz, P., Loeffler, K. & Drescher, B. (1992) Einfluss unterschiedlicher Haltungsverfahren und Bewungsmoeglichkeiten auf die Spongiosastruktur der Rippen sowie Brustund Lendenwirbel von Versuchs-und Fleischkaninchen. *Tieraerztliche Umschau.*

43. Fay, R.R. (1988). Hearing in Vertebrates. A Psychophysics Data Book. ISBN 0–9618559–0–9. Winnetka, Illinois: Hill, Fay Associates.

44. Refinements in Rabbit Husbandry; Second Report of the BVA AWF/FRAME/RSPCA/UFAW Joint Working Group on Refinement Laboratory Animals (1993) 27: 301–329.

45. Canadian Council on Animal Care (1984): Guide to the Care and use of Experimental Animals volume 2: 103–112.

46. UFAW Handbook on The Care and Management of Laboratory Animals Edited by T. Poole, 6th Edition 1987: Harlow: Longman Scientific and Technical.

47. Scharmann, W. (1991). Improved Housing of Mice, Rats and Guinea Pigs: A contribution to the refinement of animal experiments Alternatives to Laboratory Animals 19: 108–114.

48. MacArthur, J.A. (1987). The Dog. pp 456–475 In: (T. Poole ed.), The UFAW Handbook on the Care and Management of Laboratory Animals: 6th ed., Harlow: Longman Group, U.K. Ltd.

49. Hubrecht, R.C., Serpell, J.A. & Poole, T.B. (1992). Correlates of pen size and housing conditions on the behaviour of kennelled dogs. Applied Animal Behaviour Science 34: 365–383.

50. Hetts, S., Clark, J.D., Calpin, J.P., Arnold, C.E. & Mateo, J.M. (1992). Influence of housing conditions on beagle behaviour, Applied Animal Behaviour Science 37: 345–361.

51. Hubrecht, R.C. (1993). A comparison of social and environmental enrichment methods for laboratory housed dogs. Applied Animal Behaviour Science 37: 345–361.

52. Fox, M.W. & Spencer, J.W. (1969). Exploratory Behaviour in the dog: Experiential or age dependent, Developmental Psychobiology 2: 68–74.

53. Carlstead, K., Brown, J.L., Strawn, W. (1993). Behavioral and physiological correlates of stress in laboratory cats, Applied Animal Behaviour Science 38: 143–158.

54. IPS International Guidelines for the Acquisition, Care and Breeding of Non Human Primates – Codes of Practice 1–3 – (1988) PRIMATE REPORT 25 p 3–27. Prepared by the Captive Care Committee, International Primatological Society.

55. Canadian Council on Animal Care (1984): Guide to the Care and Use of Experimental Animals Volume 2 p 53–56.

56. Quail Production – MAFF/ADAS Leaflet – M.P.S., Haywood 1981.

57. Aho, W.A., Wilson, W.O., Siopes, T.D., (1969) Brooding Temperatures for Coturnix. Poult Sci. 48: 1170–2.

58. Gerken, M. and Mills A.D., Welfare of Domestic Quail – In Proceedings of Fourth European Symposium on Poultry Welfare by C.J. Savory and B.O. Hughes (1993) Universities Federation for Animal Welfare.

59. Sittman, K., Abplanalp H., Abbott U.K., (1971). Extended storage of quail, chicken and turkey eggs. 2. Embryonic abnormalities and the inheritance of twinning in quail. Poult, Sci. 50: 714–22.

Printed in the United Kingdom for HMSO.
Dd.5063552, C50, 1/95, 3398/3B, 5673, 310693.